VIKINGS, SCOTS AND SCRAELINGS

BY THE SAME AUTHOR:

HOME IS A TENT

WHITE HORIZONS

DUE NORTH

SIMPSON THE OBSTETRICIAN

For Children:

GREENLAND SUMMER

VIKINGS, SCOTS AND SCRAELINGS

by

MYRTLE SIMPSON

LONDON
VICTOR GOLLANCZ LTD
1977

ISBN 0 575 02208 6

For Bruce
my second son

Printed in Great Britain by
The Camelot Press Ltd, Southampton

LIST OF ILLUSTRATIONS

Following page 64

Discovered grave: Viking or Scraeling
Eric's fjord
Rory Simpson map-reading
Bones lying in Eric the Red's byre: Eric's fjord
Robin and Rona at the waterfall, Eric the Red's fjord
Scraeling in kayak, Narssaq
Eskimo eating boiled seal meat, Narssaq
Hvalsey church, the site of the famous last wedding; Myrtle, Rory and Robin Simpson in canoe
Hvalsey church: Rona
Viking ruins near Hvalsey
Myrtle, Robin and Rory at Igaliko fjord

Following page 128

Robin brings cod from the fjord for supper
Two Scots and five Scraelings
Rounding SW. cape between Eric's fjord and Igaliko: Myrtle, Robin and Rory
Viking storehouse—"fortification" on map—Igaliko fjord
Myrtle with Eskimo friend fixing canoes on to carrier: Igaliko settlement
Family camp at Eric's fjord
At Igaliko settlement
Igaliko fjord
Rona
Robin
Rory

VIKINGS, SCOTS AND SCRAELINGS

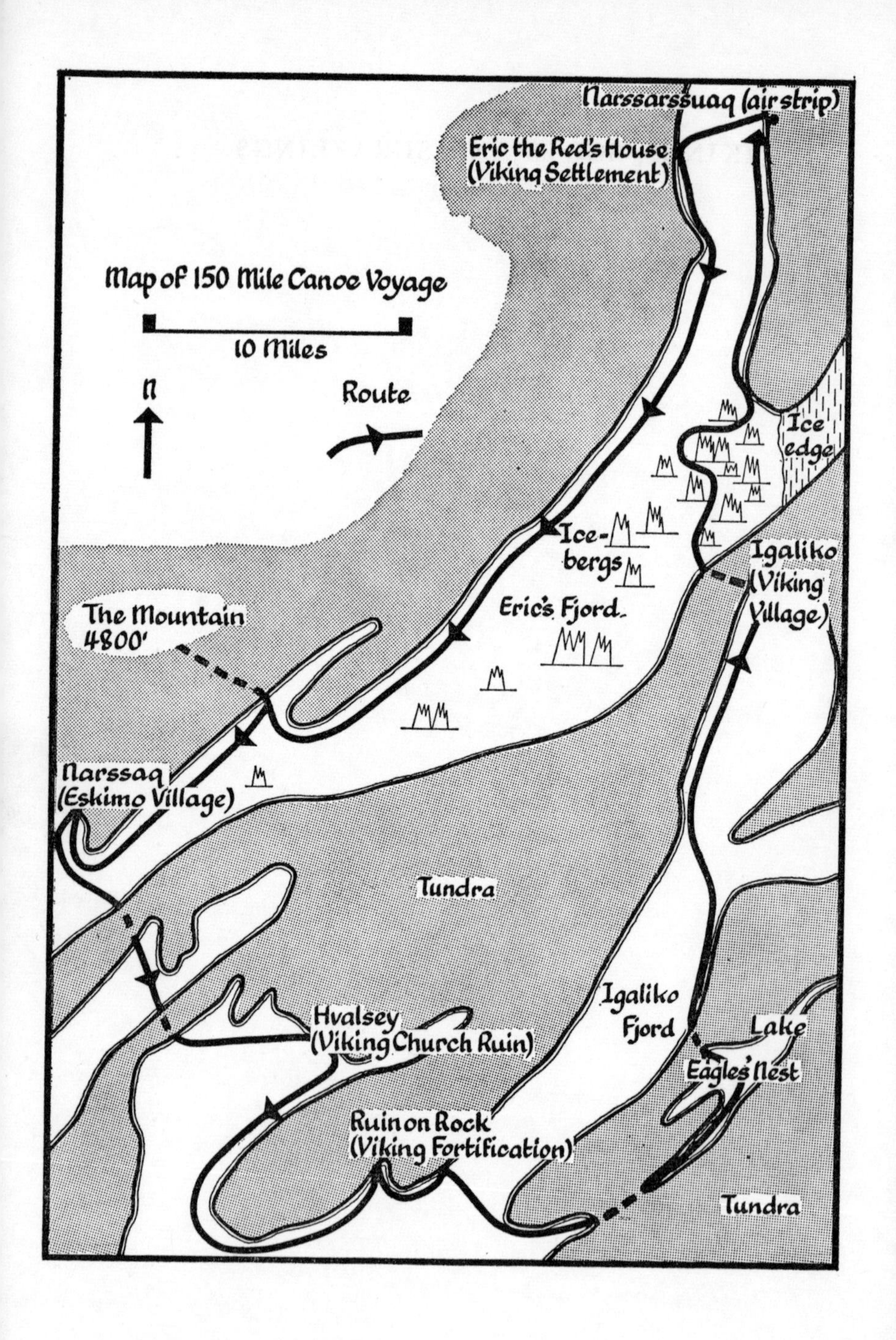
Narssarssuaq (air strip)
Eric the Red's House
(Viking Settlement)
Map of 150 Mile Canoe Voyage
10 Miles
N
Route
Ice edge
Ice-bergs
Igaliko
(Viking Village)
Eric's Fjord
The Mountain
4800'
Narssaq
(Eskimo Village)
Tundra
Igaliko Fjord
Lake
Hvalsey
(Viking Church Ruin)
Eagles' Nest
Ruin on Rock
(Viking Fortification)
Tundra

I

Whatever happened to the Vikings? There were thousands of them farming in South Greenland for hundreds of years. Certainly enough in 1408 to hold a wedding at Hvalsey, near Julianahaab, just round the corner from Cape Farewell. A large number of people were in the church and all seemed well with the settlement. Then they vanished; and nobody yet knows why.

The account of the wedding came in a letter written by a priest and "posted" from Iceland in 1414. Unfortunately the information is vague but the following facts can be extracted. Two ministers, Andresson and Halvardssen certified that they had read the banns on three consecutive Sundays for the bride and groom, and, as no one had raised any objection, they were pronounced man and wife in the Hvalsey Church on the Sunday after Cross Mass, which means 16 September. The couple's name was Olafson, but the bride would have been known by her own name of Bjornsdottir; still a custom in Iceland to this day. The priests claimed that they had been present at the ceremony. Of them it is known that they had left Norway in 1406 bound for Iceland; but they had been put off course and landed in Greenland, where they had stayed for four years. They returned to Norway in 1410 and only one is reported to have gone to Iceland. The letter was sealed at Skaga Fjord in 1414 so presumably the sender arrived sometime after 1411 but before 1414. Whenever, this is the last dated communication between Greenland and Scandinavia in mediaeval times.

Nothing seemed to have upset the peace of that autumn Sunday and from the legal point of view nothing was amiss: the banns had been read and there were relations to testify that everything was in order. There was no sign that the community was falling apart. Why was it then that when communication was eventually re-established between Europe and Greenland, there were no Vikings left? What had happened? Bad weather? A scourge of caterpillars that had devastated the crops? Measles? Murder? The clues must be there held in suspense by the crisp, cold air. Many academics have formed theories, working on odd references to the Greenland settlements in various sagas and reports. Blame has been placed on the Roman Catholic Church, which seems to have failed in its duty to the Norse population on the southern tip of Greenland: after very close ties, the newly appointed bishops had apparently no intention of leaving the mainland of Europe to travel to their northern dioceses. This must have put the local priests at a loss and caused much worry and lack of confidence. From them the feeling of unease would have spread to the settlers who were left to their devices, morally as much as physically. So long as conditions remained stable, there is no reason why the Norsemen's economy, based on farming, should not have prospered. But, supposing the conditions deteriorated? With the Scandinavian connection lost, their way of life could well have been overcome by the environment.

Archaeological evidence proves that the Scandinavians lived on till after 1480. Clothes of the type in fashion in Burgundy after 1450 have been found. These were in a remarkable state of preservation, which leads to the conclusion that temperatures, when they were placed in the graves of their wearers, must have been much lower than now. Excavations showed that the climate deteriorated and the soil became frostbound to such a depth that the warmth of the summer sun could only thaw the top few inches.

Anatomists too have thrown in their evidence as to why the Vikings disappeared. It seems that the most recent graves belonged to a people of a degenerate and doomed physical type. Their bones have been compared to those from other mediaeval remains found in European churchyards. Whilst the latter showed that some degree of malnutrition was normal during the Middle Ages, famine being quite common and people lacking in many vitamins for most of the year, the Greenlanders were shown to have been living well below the norm.

In November 1415, Eric VII of Scandinavia sent reports to

the English king, Henry V, complaining that English traders had sailed unlawfully to the islands of Orkney, Shetland and Faroe. King Eric also alluded to other Atlantic islands, and it is apparent that he wished to assert his sovereignty over these outlying places. Henry V seems to have accepted the fact that the islands belonged to Scandinavia, although English navigation in northern waters continued. The success of these traders was often based on rough methods; murder and fire were everyday happenings. English assaults were recorded as having taken place in Iceland throughout the fifteenth century. Greenland itself is not mentioned in these reports, but there is much allusion in the ships' logs to being driven off course to Greenland while bound for Iceland and Norway. A fifteenth-century papal letter also complains of attacks on the Scandinavian settlements by "barbarians and heathens". However, although Rome considered the English highly uncivilized, this letter could be referring to attacks by the Stone Age Eskimos, who were migrating from the north and spreading along the coast of west and south Greenland.

It was definitely the Englishman, Martin Frobisher, who rediscovered Greenland in 1576. He was actually sailing to find the north-west passage to China and when he reached Greenland he thought he had arrived at the site of the mythical island of Friesland which figured on the earliest maps. As a result, the southernmost point of Greenland was placed far to the north on Frobisher's maps, a mistake that led to the disasters of the eighteenth century when many ships were wrecked on the impenetrable coast of eastern Greenland. Frobisher brought home an Eskimo but no Viking.

Another Englishman, John Davies, was a more knowledgeable navigator who visited Greenland on three voyages between 1585 and 1587. He charted the newly discovered areas, giving his name to the Davies Strait. He also met some Eskimos. To please them, Davies had taken ashore his ship's orchestra which won over the locals who were then prepared to trade. Davies noted that everything was made from sealskin: high boots, breeches and gloves, all carefully sewn and well tanned. That meeting ended with a game of football between the sailors and the Eskimos. The Scandinavians did not return to the shores of Greenland until 1605 when the first Danish expedition, commanded by Admiral Godske Lindenow, reached the west coast.

The fate of Lindenow's Scandinavian predecessors has often puzzled me. I have long wanted to discover the facts and to travel the way of the Vikings: to camp among the ruins of their farms and early settlements; to travel as they did in a small boat up and down the fjords, answering to the weather and the tide. I had been to Greenland many times before, but never to the far south. I therefore decided to make the journey and to take three of my children with me; my husband, Hugh, would join us halfway through our journey, once he was free of a conference in America. Robin, 14, would have to act as "Dad"; Rona, 13, would have to help with looking after the youngest, Rory, aged 5.

We caught up with the dawn as the plane escaped the rain of West Scotland, where we live, and soared north over the clouds. It was 3 a.m. when we landed in Iceland. I felt very low as I staggered out of the airport at Keflavik with the children. The landscape was desolate: black with lava waste. "No wonder they want their fish," I said to the children, "they have so little else." We had a day to spare before our onward connection, so we lay in a hot spring with only our heads poking out to be refreshed by the constant rain. Later we clambered aboard the archaic DC6 for Greenland wearing our boots and our only clothes for the next five weeks. With two canoes in our luggage, weight was at a premium. Our pockets bulged with bags of sugar and books. Rory clutched his hand luggage: the heavy frying pan, and primus loaded with forbidden paraffin. But what is the traveller to do? Newfangled cookers are heavier and need constant supplies of fuel that can only be purchased in sophisticated environments; and in any case the old-fashioned primus gives out more heat per unit. All we needed had to be with us aboard the plane. If I had forgotten anything it was just too bad and we would have to do without. As soon as we stepped off the plane in Greenland we would be on our own and completely self-supporting.

The plane droned slowly across the Atlantic. There were some American tourists aboard. It is not only the intrepid explorer who travels north these days; money, too, can buy you the choice of a polar bear or a walrus in your viewfinder and a go at crunching through the pack ice in the crystal clear air of the Arctic summer. It has to be the summer, as only then can the Arctic supply the back-up needed to take wealthy tourists to parts of the world with few hotels, no sewerage, T-bone steaks, and certainly no canned entertainments.

I felt depressed as I looked at our fellow passengers. It must be a good thing, I tried to persuade myself, for people to flock to the high Arctic. There is so much space. But actually the vastness is very vulnerable to the ravages of the tourist. The thin soil will not stand many feet trudging over it—200 years are needed to renew the tundra after the passing of one tracked vehicle. The modern ecologists, particularly American and Canadian, say that there is no room, in fact, for man in the Arctic. I disagree with them, for the Eskimo has hung on for 2,000 years; so why shouldn't modern man have a look? But the people surrounding me would surely be happier in the Caribbean or surfing off the Florida coast; or was I maligning them? Could they really be longing, as I was, for the brush of the Arctic wind on the face, the marvellous stillness and silence of the far north, the limitless views in a land where there is often no horizon? I have spent many, many months of my life camping far north of the Arctic circle, in all the Arctic countries of the old and new worlds. I have crossed right over the Greenland Ice Cap on skis; attempted to reach the North Pole on another journey; have lived with the Eskimos of Canada as well as of Greenland, comparing their way of life with that of the Lapps of Europe. I love these northern people, their freshness, their uncomplicated way of life where the values are assessed by the weather.

The American tourist sitting next to me was avid for information, and I explained that the people he would see in Greenland had originally come from Mongolia, the first Eskimos arriving about 3000 BC. The land was warmer then, higher above the tide and there was more grass to walk on; the people followed the Musk Ox. These earliest settlers were followed through the ages by those with bows and arrows, then came others with harpoons and boats. We know that the weather changed because the shape of the old houses was altered. As the climate became warmer so the dwellings widened: the fireplace became insignificant, and the floor not so deeply set. The American was writing all this down in his notebook. Heavens, I thought, I hope my facts are correct. Now he fumbled in his pocket and produced a dictaphone to record my potted lesson on Eskimo migration. No wonder there was a Watergate scandal! But I knew that the modern Greenlander would be genuinely pleased with his interest, would produce his bead work and show off his skill with skins. The tourist can be useful in appreciating native crafts. A standard is set and old skills retained. It is easier to buy a rubber boot from a store, but why not make one from skin and enjoy showing it off to next summer's tourists? Better by far to spend the winter evenings sewing than hanging around the pub. Modern ways result in hours of formerly unknown leisure. Filling them is a great problem to the unsophisticated—this curse of Western culture is as dangerous as measles or TB.

My thoughts were interrupted as my eye caught a glint of white below: pack ice! The mountains of the east coast of Greenland reared up. The pilot swung low to please his cargo of tourists. Dazzling white snow and black, black rock. The coast-line was hostile, mountainous, with naked granite cliffs and snow peaks flattening out into the inland ice. I thought about the Vikings who, after their fantastic voyage across the north Atlantic, desperately felt their way along the edge of the ice and rock in their open boats, frantically looking for somewhere to land, somewhere green for their sheep, somewhere uninhabited and empty, offering them homes for their families. They didn't know, of course, that the Eskimos were already there: food gatherers and hunters up and down the coast, on the move, catching a living off the ice and land, sleeping in round houses only a few feet tall, with, by this time, a sunken passage to the outside. It is this race that has blended with the

European voyagers since the fourteenth century to make the Greenlanders of today. They are a lively, energetic people, full of purpose, and interested in taking an active part in the modern world—even to the extent of running the country as an independent state and not as part of Denmark, as it is officially today. No naïve, noble savage perhaps, but not the hopeless drunken Eskimo that one can see in the North American Arctic where the people have been encouraged to "integrate", which is another word for giving up their own culture, beliefs and way of life.

Now we were flying over the ice cap. The startling white gave way to brown, and suddenly we were there: Narssarssuaq. The plane swept out over the green water to bring itself in line with the tarmac, which only points in one direction. "It's the Danish airstrip," I shouted to my neighbour, "but did you know that it was the US base during the war, built as a refuelling stop before your planes continued on to bomb Europe? See those houses," I pointed down at some decaying-looking buildings of grey concrete; "do you know what those were for?" He shook his head. "They were built to house seriously wounded GIs. The men were hidden to protect the US public."

"No," he said incredulously.

"Yes, that's a fact," I answered. "It was to keep the reality of war from you." There was no time for further comment; the plane juddered as its wheels made contact with the ground.

As usual, the milling mass of people tried to get out at once. Being an old hand I wanted to wait until last, but Rory and Rona were already pushing and shoving for space in the narrow corridor. "Come on, Mum," they shouted over their shoulders. "Hurry, hurry. Let's get going." Reluctantly I joined the pushing and shoving. I clambered down the steps and took a deep breath. It was marvellous; just as I had expected. I felt alive, every sense sharpened, my mind alert. What a contrast to the social-security world of Britain today. I'm half asleep at home, and feel the family unit threatened on all sides. Here we were going to do something together: look for Viking remains. We stood aside as the tourists grappled with their baggage. I felt superior. Thank Heavens, I thought, I am self-sufficient. I can live here without the back-up of the hotel. Already they were fussing, wondering where they were going and how, who would be there to show them the way and what they were going to eat. Would there be hot water and the beds comfortable? We waited for them to be shepherded into a bus and driven off to a building very similar to the one their war-wounded fathers had been taken to 30 years before. It is amazing what paint, and a clever Danish interior decorator can do with a slab of cement!

I had an introduction to the base-leader, and there was no mistaking him as he came up. A Dane, completely at home and relaxed in the environment. He had been in Greenland for many long years by choice, not wooed by extra money as with so many Canadian officials. He loved the way of life and was an authority on the local birds and flowers. He helped us collect our luggage and gather it together at the edge of the airstrip which ran out into the water of the fjord. We could go no further until we had erected our canoes.

Somehow, I had imagined that I would not be faced with coping just yet—nothing for it, though, but to empty out the canvas bags on to the ground. The bundle of plywood looked like firewood. The Dane and some Greenlanders gathered round to see what this pile of sticks could possibly turn into. I was slightly agitated, always having left this job to my husband. But Robin seemed to know what was what, and it was great to be told what to do by my eldest boy. We matched pieces of red-ended wood to pieces of blue, and, gradually, the skeleton of a canoe-shaped object began to take form. We have used this type of canoe on many journeys to Greenland. They are looked upon as rather old fashioned by the fibreglass-slalom brigade of today; but there is no better craft for family touring on the sea, as I have proved time and time again. The "Tyne Sports" was originally made by an English boat-building firm for a journey in Arctic Finland by the owner and a few friends. Since then his canoes have been all over the Arctic, across the Atlantic, and many times around the islands of the west coast of Scotland. Their great advantage is that there is room for a lot of luggage, so long as it is carefully stowed under the bows. The length of the canoe means that it rides well in a rough sea, and it is extraordinarily stable provided the weight is kept low. The boat is built along the lines of the genuine Eskimo kayak, with a superstructure of wood, and then a skin of rubberized canvas or, these days, of plastic. Robin and Rona were now stretching out this cover, and my job was carefully to place the skeleton inside and put pressure on the middle until all the wood was covered. The Greenlanders were incredulous, and admiration was even apparent in the eyes of the Danish base-leader who had reckoned until that minute that he had seen most things in his long life in the outback. There were too many people about to test our canoe: nothing for it but to load up. We pushed the bags of flour and oats, dried milk and matches into the cockpit, and underneath the bows and stern. I was to be the captain in canoe with Rory as my crew; Robin and Rona were to be of the other.

"Now," said the Danish leader, realizing that we were really on our way and not likely to be on his hands for the next five weeks, "watch out for the wind from the west. We call it the *fohn.* It's very dangerous, as it comes up extremely fast out of a clear sky. It whips the fjord into a fine scale sea in no time at all." He shook me by the hand. Rory stepped gingerly in, and I pushed the canoe away from the shore before lowering myself in, trying hard not to wet my feet at this early stage of our voyage. We sat slightly off-shore while Rona and Robin argued as to who was to get in first.

"Me, me," said Rona, "I am not going to get my feet wet."

"No, I have to," said Robin. "You can't hold the boat still without it rubbing on the rocks."

I hoped the Greenlanders could not understand their bickering. I have never seen Eskimo children argue, or even fight. They push and shove and compete, but are always ready with a laugh rather than an angry word.

We were away. We had packed the boats in a hurry and I was trying not to make a fool of myself so close to the shore. When I did look round we were already out of sight, the airstrip had vanished behind a boss of rock; we were completely on our own. A great wave of exhilaration swept over me. I yelled, waved my paddle in the air and then began to use it furiously. "Look out," yelled Rory, "you're wetting me." He leant backwards to pull up his hood. His paddle slipped out of his hands and he reached out to collect it. "Watch out," I shouted, "we're nearly over." Robin and Rona swept past us, fired with the same enthusiasm as I was. Our first iceberg lay between us and the main fjord, to remind us that we really were in the Arctic. "Let's camp as soon as we can," I shouted to Robin. "I'm much too tired to go far today." The rock extended straight into the sea with no shore, but it fell back after a while into a bay with a shingle beach. A little stream tumbled into the sea and, just beyond the spit, I lowered my feet into the icy water before the canoe touched: rubbing the plastic-coated canvas on the stones could wear it away in no time. Protected by the shelving beach was a small flat piece of land, just large enough for the tent. Soon we had it up with all our goods and chattels strewn around outside. I just had enough energy to shake out our bright red sleeping bag, carefully constructed for us many years ago as a "family" bag. Mum and Dad had one end and the kids the other. This time, though, it was Rona and I who snuggled up, with Robin and Rory shoving their feet between ours, jostling for space in the middle. This single bag is far warmer than having one each, and, of course, infinitely lighter. It is the answer to light-weight camping. I was glad that I was not one of the early Polar explorers. Nansen described sharing such a bag with four large smelly-footed companions wearing sea boots!

I slept the night through, far better than the last few weeks at home where I had woken up constantly, worrying about my ability to take on this voyage alone. Here, I was so comfortable that I could barely stir myself to peep out of the tent. Rory beat me to it. "Manc," he said, and quickly zipped up the flap and snuggled in once more. An hour later we surfaced again to a fine drizzle and low mist. I put the primus together and soon had it roaring into life.

"Oh," wailed Rona, "the marmalade has exploded in the

camera bag. I didn't eat it on the plane as I thought it might be useful."

I scraped it off the lens and spread it with my finger on the last slice of Glasgow bread.

"I'm going fishing," said Robin. "Come on, Rory, I'll need you too."

Knowing the fjords in the south to be stiff with cod we had brought a mackerel-type fishing line, with four feathered hooks and a weight. Robin lowered this down just off shore, and, no sooner down, than he was pulling the line in with a flashing silvery body struggling on the first hook. Further in and another fish appeared, and another. "Three in one go," he yelled to me. He lowered it in again and got two more. The five fish were thrashing around in the bottom of the canoe as I helped him ashore.

"Gut them," I said.

"Oh, Mum," he answered, horrified, "that's your job."

I realized it probably was. Nothing for it but to start hacking off heads. "Have another look for that sharp knife," I shouted to Rona. "It must be somewhere." I meant to bring it specially, and remember putting it out at the kitchen sink before we left home. But the only one we could find was a blunt one.

The Greenland cod has a black body lining. It's very neat inside and the innards fall out easily. It seemed a shame not to eat the fish now that we had caught them, and I felt the urge for a driftwood fire. There was plenty strewn around the high-water mark: pieces of fish box, planks, poles, branches and roots of trees that never grew in Greenland. The Umbellifera angelica grew to about two feet just at the edge of the beach. Its dead branches looked ideal as a firelighter. Sure enough, it lit with one match. We gathered round and perched our frying pan on top of the sticks. The fish quickly flaked and disintegrated. I crisped it up while the kids searched for flat pieces of wood to use as plates. Delicious! "I could live off this," said Robin. "You'll have to," I answered. "I only brought basics, like flour and dried milk, you know. Meat will have to be cod." "Oh, it's just great," echoed Rory. "I don't mind in the least." We burnt the plates as additional fuel and settled round watching the final blaze. Scrub willow grew on the lower slopes of the bluffs behind us. I wandered off, gaining a little height. There was the dark green of the juniper with lots of berries, an Arctic poppy the pink of willow herb, and, as I gained more height, this gave way to single stems of draba and tufts of sea pink. "Can I eat these peas?" shouted Rory coming up with a stem of Arctic japonica. Sure enough, the seeds looked readily edible, but I had no idea whether they really were.

There was a lightness in the sky on the far side of the fjord. "That's the ice blink," I explained to Rona.

"It isn't," she said, "it just means it's clearing up."

Everything Rona said these days was punctuated with clicks from her newly-acquired brace. It was driving me mad already. The worst thing about living in a tent is that everyone's failings rub on one's nerves. "You should like people in spite of their failings," Hugh always said. His experience of three years in the Antarctic, living with a few men in a very confined space, hemmed in by darkness and snowdrifts, had forced him to this conclusion. I, however, am not so stoical and am more aware of my children's failings than other people's, and even less tolerant.

Teeming, driving rain now drove us into the tent. I was glad. I dug into my bag and brought out *Dombey and Son.* This is just the occasion for Dickens—in a tent with time to fill. His punctilious detail, and involved plot with numerous story lines, is ideal in such a situation.

"Clear enough to cross," announced Robin a few hours later. It was still raining but quite calm. The main worry was the three-mile crossing of the fjord.

"Couldn't we just stay here till Dad comes?" asked Rory.

"Of course not," I said crossly, "we've got to be half way through our journey before he arrives. Come on now, we can manage perfectly well by ourselves."

I had no more confidence than he, but busily began packing everything into long, narrow, nylon bags. These we then dropped into larger, black, plastic bags given to us by the Glasgow Corporation during our recent garbage strike. Who would have thought that such convenience would have come out of the union's demand for extra pay? I chivvied on the children. With waterproof trousers and cagoules down to our eyes we were well protected from the rain. We squashed the load into the canoes, then wedged ourselves around the bags. The tide was receding as we paddled out of the sheltered bay. Rory paddled too deep and nearly tipped. I could feel the tide. On and on, chunks of ice signified our progress.

"Paddle left," I shouted to Rory, suddenly becoming aware of an imminent collision.

"Now, which is left again?" he queried, waving his hand.

I cursed him loudly and paddled frantically on one side myself. This difficulty over, Rory and I now settled down to a rhythm. We had a long way to go.

"Who were these Vikings anyway?" shouted Rory over his shoulder. "Why did they come here? What have they got to do with Greenland?"

"Well," I began, "the story begins in 970 when a man was made to leave his country, Norway, with his son, because he had committed a crime. In those days instead of being sent to prison people were banished from their homeland as a punishment. Father and son emigrated to Iceland where they had relations. They settled in the north-west at a place that we have visited, the Horn Peninsula. When the father died, his son Erik, who was known as Erik the Red, married a girl called Thjodhild, the daughter of a rich farmer. Although it was Erik the Red who first settled in Greenland and thus became famous, his wife, Thjodhild, was herself equally influential; which is strange when one considers the status of women in the Middle Ages. But in those very difficult times all the Viking women had to be amazingly resourceful, for the men were at sea for years on end. Icelandic sagas teem with accounts of long sea voyages. Most were trading expeditions, but in those days it was only a short step from barter to battle, and a trader had to have his arms at the ready. In the ninth century there was a constant shuttle of Viking long-boats between Scandinavia and the

Shetlands, the Orkneys, Ireland, the Faroes and Iceland. And whilst the men were at sea the women farmed, made decisions and dealt with all the problems that arose; thus they assumed a position of authority in the Norse way of life.

"It had been a good choice to marry Thjodhild, since her mother lived on good land behind the Breidi Fjord. Erik moved there, settled, and began to clear the land. But he was soon in trouble. It is recorded that his serfs sent an avalanche down onto another man's house. The man's kinsmen then killed Erik's serfs and Erik had to avenge himself by retaliating. Under Icelandic law he was exiled from the area, and he was forced to move to the islands in the estuary. Thinking that he would not be there for long he lent some of his belongings to a friend. However, when he decided to settle there permanently, the friend refused to hand back the possessions. It resulted in a quarrel which split the district into two parties: one supporting Erik's rights to ownership, and the other his old friend. Several people were killed and Erik was hauled in front of the local government or 'Thing'. The jury outlawed him and his accomplices for three years. Where to go? Norway and now Iceland were forbidden him. He decided to fill in the time by sailing west, to follow up the rumour that had been brought back by a Norwegian sailor, Gunnbjorn, some 50 years earlier. Gunnbjorn had related that during a storm he had been driven off course, first south and then west of Iceland, when he had sighted the coast of a new land. Was this rumour true? Erik set off on the 65th parallel late in the summer of 982.

"Sure enough, Gunnbjorn had been right, and Erik found himself on the coast of a land of black rock and white ice. He turned and sailed south with the land mass on his right, rounding what we call today Cape Farewell: he found himself in a green land full of animals and fish, birds and space. Nobody was there. Islands, deep fingers of fjords, rolling hills, and beyond them the Inland Ice responsible for the rivers and lakes. Best of all, however, were the grassy slopes and scrub strewn valleys; they were his for the taking with no fighting or arguing involved! For three years he explored the region with his crew. He found foxes, reindeer, seal, whales and fish.

"With his period of banishment over, Erik determined to return quickly to Iceland for his wife and then come back for good. On his arrival he found the country ravaged by a cruel famine and the people facing a bleak future. So, when he recounted the stories of the green land beyond the sea, many people wanted to accompany him. Twenty-five ships were filled and soon they were off again. The new followers were people from the western parts of Iceland and they rallied round Erik with all their property—their cattle, arms and implements, and their serfs—and, of course, their wives and children. Mostly they were prepared to move on as they were dissatisfied with the conditions in Iceland and they were anxious to try their fortunes further west, tempted by Erik's praise of his new land.

"Headed by Erik's ship, the heavily laden fleet left west Iceland drawing a good deal of water. On board one of the boats was a Christian from Scotland. This man wrote a poem describing the appalling storms that they had to cope with on their voyage. One such storm was so frightful that it could perhaps have been volcanic activity that threw the sea up into such incredible chaos. The poem reads: 'It is as if all the gales and waves that can be found in that sea draw up into three lines so that they form three waves altogether. These three waves circumscribed the entire ocean and you do not know whether to sail and they are taller than mountains and it is but seldom that anybody gets out of the sea once he has been in it.' Twelve ships foundered. Half open, and so heavily laden, it is not surprising. What relief, therefore, they must have felt when at last they sighted land and made the green shores of the fjord. Erik knew exactly where he was heading; although there was an old Viking custom of letting the gods decide where one settled by throwing wooden pillars overboard and landing where they were washed ashore."

This was the place where we were now heading in our little open canoes: the bright green of Erik's farm enticing us through the grey rainy smir. "It's clearing up," called Rory, pushing back his cagoule hood. Sure enough the rain clouds were being driven away by a strong wind blowing straight into our faces. Already the waves were slapping over the bows, flowing over the coaming. "Hard work," yelled Robin pulling ahead of me. He and Rona in their canoe offered less resistance to the wind. My arms were tired pushing with all my strength against the wind. Half an hour of it and the far shore still looked no nearer. "Paddle, paddle," I kept urging Rory, needing his help. We must have inched forward because, at last, we were in the lee, sheltered by the shadow of the cliffs. We headed straight for a little bay and beached the canoes in a cove short of the farm which was now out of sight. It was a storm beach. Clambering up to a ledge we smelled the scent of the wild thyme which hung in the air, and found orchids, harebells, bartsia and gentians among the shrubs of the arctic birch. The sun glinted on crystals in the bed-rock. Is this what it felt like for the Vikings after their voyage, I wondered. Crossing the Atlantic in an open boat stashed with horses, cows, goats, women and children must have been awful.

Their ship-of-all-work, the true ocean-goer, was called the "half ship" or "knorr". It was broader in the beam, deeper in the water and of a higher freeboard than the conventional Viking long-boat. It was constructed almost entirely of oak, though the sixteen pairs of oars were made of pine and so regulated in length that they struck the water at the same time. They were kept in place by means of rowlocks. The mast, too, was of pine, probably about 35 feet tall with the big square sail made of strips of heavy woollen material strengthened by rope. A huge chunk of oak supported the mast with a cunningly designed socket for the enormous upright. The Viking ship could be sailed across, and even near the wind. This was largely due to the use of a kind of removable boom whose heavy end was seated in a socket abeam of the mast, while its lighter end was fitted to the forward end of the sail to keep it taut and drawing when the ship was sailing on the wind. The ship was steered by a side rudder, fastened to the starboard quarter. Recently, Captain Magnus Anderson crossed the Atlantic in a replica of such a ship, and he reported that this side rudder was the clearest proof of the Vikings' great ability at shipbuilding, and goes far to explain how they managed to cross the ocean on their long voyage. He reported that the side rudder could be managed single-handed in all weather with the help of only one small line. The Vikings also kept a small ship's boat aboard, which was about twenty feet long. The knorr itself would be tented for sleeping, the tents being constructed of spare sail material, of which there was plenty. With its large sail and numerous oars the ship could penetrate and manoeuvre in the narrow and ice-filled fjords.

At the time of the Viking voyages, of course, the sailors had neither compass nor chart. How then did the Norwegian and Icelandic skippers make their way confidently and accurately from, say, Bergen in Norway to Angmugsslik on the east coast of Greenland? It is accepted that their method was to commit the ship to a latitude of sailing. This was done by moving up the coast of Norway until a particular landmark was reached, and then striking out into the open sea, counting the days and passing north of the Shetlands and south of the Faroes at a prescribed distance. In clear weather and with a following wind, this part of the journey would take about seven days; it would take almost as long again before they sighted the east coast of Greenland, about 80 miles north of Cape Farewell. These sailors knew the value of the sun and stars and they had the art of ready reckoning and the use of a line to plumb the ocean's depths. In a good day's sailing they could cover 120 miles or more. But how did they definitely fix their latitude? That they were able to do so is certain, for marked sticks, which were used to give the mariner an indication of his latitude in comparison with a known place, have been found. Other methods they employed were to observe the location of the mid-day sun and the measurement of the shadow cast at noon; or to calculate the height of the Pole Star above the horizon, expressed in terms of a man's own armspan. A half-round disc of wood has been discovered, too, which was perhaps a more sophisticated division of the horizon. The complete disc would rotate round a pin, or, perhaps, float in a bowl of water with a piece of magnetite at the bottom: a kind of original compass.

How many people were aboard those ships? It seems from

sagas that 35 was probably a likely crew. The weight of their ships was supposed to be about twenty metric tons, enough to carry Erik and his family through the Greenland waters to where we were ourselves.

We had pitched our tent on the only level camp site, a few feet above the sea. We were surrounded by a meadow of flowers. I was so thankful to be safely on this side of the fjord. We had just made the only really dangerous open sea crossing that we would be faced with before being joined by Hugh. The sun was low now, beneath the clouds, and we were bathed in a soft golden light. Rona and Rory scampered about exploring, slithering down the grassy bank on to the storm beach which was heaped with wood of all shapes and sizes—vast tree roots, boxes, poles—the flotsam and jetsam from all over Europe which had been picked up by the currents and carried northwards. "Look at my treasure," Rory shouted. It was a plastic aerosol container. As there was so much wood lying around, Robin lit a Guy Fawkes-type bonfire; we therefore had our supper in the open, just below the tent. Rory again urged me to come and see what he had found. I clambered up towards some rocks, which were extraordinarily soft and had been gouged out into bowls and caves, some of which were big enough to root around in. Growing around the rocks were the delicate little plants of the cornel berry. Some were ripe already; they squelched in our mouths, bursting with one bite of freshness. These were Rory's find. Yet another, "Look what I've found," this time from Rona below. "Do you think we can eat them?" She brought up a handful of mushrooms. I couldn't believe they really were the true domestic variety, but sure enough they peeled and smelt authentic. But I was wary of them, having once eaten the deadly amanita by mistake. It had been whilst we were travelling in Iceland, living entirely off the land. With us were three children under three years. One of them, Rona, was only two weeks old and I was feeding her myself. We were very hungry and, late at dusk with little light around, we found some mushrooms, fried them and gobbled them for supper.

They were delicious. During the night I was overcome by the most appalling sickness. Hugh was agitated, thinking that whatever had upset me would certainly upset the baby. I writhed and groaned all night. In the light of the morning we realized that the smaller, slightly yellower amanita, which does not peel, was growing unmistakably among the surrounding mushrooms. However, there was no doubt about Rona's find. The ground was littered with them; the fresh green grass was short, and the white, perfectly rounded heads of the mushrooms were poking up just above the soil. We all gathered as many as we could and took them back to the tent, thinking of the next day's breakfast.

2

When I peeped out of the tent the following morning a wheatear was hopping about outside. This little sparrow-sized bird with its white tail feathers is the most common around these parts. Lying back in the sleeping bag I could see yellow bartsia, cornel berries, harebells, gentians, stelaria, and an old Eskimo ruin; also, high above the opposite mountains, I could see a dash of white that I knew to be the ice cap. The grey scene became green as the sun filtered through the high-level clouds. A sheep was bleating, a sound I had never expected to hear in Greenland. "Is this tent yak proof?" asked Rory suddenly. "Don't be daft, you're in the wrong country," said Rona. "Anyway, it's just sheep that you can hear," I explained. It was the Vikings that first brought them to Greenland, of course; but now the Danish government has tried to encourage the Eskimos, or Greenlanders as they prefer to be called, to tend the sheep. In the old days the Greenland families were always on the move, following the seal and the reindeer. But now the government tries to make them settle down and live in villages. So, of course, they need to grow their own food, and farm like Europeans. "I can't imagine Greenlanders making good sheep farmers," I said to Robin. "From what I know of them they just wouldn't be able to resist killing the sheep. Anything that moves or flies is fair game as far as they are concerned," I added. "To live completely off the land has always been their way of life."

I remembered the mushrooms and crawled out of the sleeping bag. I was wearing jeans over woollen long-johns, both of which I had been sleeping in, so getting up was easy. Gathering more wood we found some puff balls just at the right stage for eating. So long as they are small and have not yet "puffed" they are safe and delicious. My favourite way of cooking them is in the oven with a blob of marg on top; they turn into a sort of marshmallow. But all we could do with our find was to fry them.

"You'll have to be careful when slicing them," I said to Rona, "because they tend to collapse."

"I wish we had some bacon," she wailed.

"Oh," said Rory, "you've got moana-tisus."

"That's quite true," confirmed Robin, "you're not meant to be an explorer. I wish you hadn't come."

Her face crumpled up and she began to cry. "It's not that, I'm just longing for Dad."

True enough, we had always travelled as a family before, loving the close compact unit.

"The Vikings were great family people, too," I said. "A man stuck to his family in all circumstances and relied on them for assistance and support in time of trouble. In the Viking age swords were quickly unsheathed; Viking blood was easily roused and it was only a short step from angry words to actual fighting that might end in death. At such a time a man needed his family. For his part it was his duty to help and support them; failure brought the worst possible consequences down on his head: ostracism and outlawry. This close family unit was, of course, difficult for a peace-loving man for he would have to go along with the family if it were involved in an argument. A Viking poem, 'The Havamal', meaning 'the sayings of the high one', is full of advice on how a man could control his family and yet keep out of trouble. It urges him to cultivate friends, otherwise he might find himself alone and without help when unforeseen danger cropped up. 'A man without a friend is like a naked fir tree without bark or leaves, lonely on a barren hill.' It tells him to avoid arrogance towards less important men, to be prudent, vigilant and well behaved, as well as to make every effort to be on good terms with his in-laws! Marriages were arranged by parental agreement, sons ensuring a continuity of the name. In peace time the Viking had a strong liking for the domestic life."

"In that case," said Rona, "why didn't they stay at home in Norway? Why were they forever off in their boats?"

"Well," I answered, "as I was telling Rory during the crossing yesterday, the Vikings were great traders and that was the reason why they made so many of their voyages about northern Europe."

"But they were fighters," interrupted Robin.

"When circumstances were good," I explained, "they were happy to be traders and merchants, but when they came to undefended towns it was easy for a trader to turn pirate. There is a story of the Vikings arriving at Dorchester in England. They met a man who thought that they were merchants and he directed them to the large manor house owned by a rich aristocrat in order that they could carry out the customary trade preliminaries. However, the Vikings killed him and plundered the town. Ireland, England and France were the Vikings' source for all the good things of life. They hankered after the beautiful trappings to be found in a large country house, they longed for books, art, wealth and a civilization that they felt to be superior to their own in the far north; they were rather like the Spanish conquistadors who went to the New World and ravished Mexico and Peru. It was easy for the Vikings to take from the monasteries and churches, the coastal towns and defenceless manor houses, as well as the rich farms. It wasn't that they were better fighters or braver than the people whose land they were attacking; there was just no opposition to their surprise attacks."

Breakfast over, we left the tent standing and slithered down the bank and crossed the shingle to the canoes, to move round to Erik's farm. There was little colour, but, as we rounded the headland, the sun sparkled on an area of rich green. We knew this to be the site of the first settlement. A great pong of fish wafted out to us from several little houses dotted along the shore. We beached the canoes at a small jetty and stepped over the refuse of a Greenland settlement, up to the rich pastureland of the Viking's farm. Grassy mounds took shape into the ground plan of the buildings as we drew nearer. The turf houses of Scandinavia stood for no more than 50 years, so it is not surprising that there was not much to be seen in the way of farm buildings. But, gradually, in Greenland a special technique had been developed involving the use of stone between the turfs.

The most important task confronting the first settlers from Iceland would have been to build a home. They had left their homeland in the spring, and it would have been late summer when they reached the Greenland shores. They did not have much time in which to build shelters for themselves and their livestock before the onslaught of winter. This explains the extensions and rebuilding that seems to have taken place around the original farm dwelling. Now, before our own eyes, we could see how those early people had beaten Greenland's cold and violent weather. Although it is known that the climate was consistently warmer than it is today, once the sun had left the sky for the winter the cold from the Inland Ice would have spread over the country, with the wind piercing through every crack and cranny, forcing the snow through so that small drifts formed behind every chink.

"The first thing they did was to build what is called the 'long house'," I explained to the children. It was easy for us to pick it out among the ruins. We clambered over the grassy wall and sat down inside. Rory was unimpressed, and started somersaulting off the grass into the trench below. I tried to keep his attention by telling him what the house would have been like in the early days. "That must have been the fireplace you're standing in," I told him. "It would have occupied the whole centre of the floor. They didn't cook on the fire though. Can you see any signs of cooking pits along that wall opposite the front door?"

"Yes," said Rona, "look here." There were some upright flagstones and behind them evidence of two or three separate dips in the ground. "It must have been cold," she said. "Think of the draughts."

That in fact was the main problem that the Norsemen had to face. It is interesting that their houses began to change from the traditional ones in Iceland.

"To start with, when they came to Greenland they built exactly the same as they had at home," I told them, "but they soon began to change. This house we are now in is not the original. A Danish archaeologist who was digging here found traces of an even older building below it."

"Here are the byres," said Robin, who had wandered out of the long-house. "You can still see the stones that separated the stalls for the cows."

Rory and Rona ran off to look. One of the stall stones was the shoulder-blade of a whale. It was still standing there, starkly white against the green of the lush grass around it.

"It's a funny place to have built the farm," said Rona; "look how stony it is round here. Why didn't he choose over there, where it's much more like a field?"

"Oh," I answered, "that's because every bit of soil where they could grow grass was of great importance. They had to make sure that their dwelling houses and outhouses, stables and so on, didn't take up any land that they could use. That's why they have built this on the edge of the farm and not in the middle as at home. Of course, there was more land in those days than now. Greenland has actually been sinking a couple of inches every hundred years. In their day, about a thousand years ago, the shore was much further out than now, so these gentle slopes we can see would have been bigger. Look at the view Erik must have had from this door. Anyone standing here would have been able to see for miles up and down and across the fjord. No boat could creep up on him and take him unawares."

"What do you think it was like then in the houses?" asked Rona, turning round again and looking into the rectangular-shaped hall.

"Well, the first thing they had to do was to keep warm," I said. "Look how thick the walls are, just about as wide as Rory if he were to lie down outstretched, which is about three feet. But the walls wouldn't be all that much higher than they are now. The roof would have been made of turf, held up by wooden props with a sort of criss-cross of any wood that they could find nearby as a superstructure. After a while, the turf would grow so that the roof would be very snug and would certainly keep in any heat that there was. But, of course, it would be low and dark and full of smoke once that roof was constructed. There were no chimneys, you see."

"Do you think this was a drain?" asked Robin, pointing to a stone conduit that passed from the back wall right out through the front.

"Yes," I replied, "it would carry water through. They must have had a lot of trouble with melting snow. Just think what it would have been like—they had far more snow falling here in the south of Greenland, than further north where it was colder." However, there was no drain that I could see from the byre. "Just imagine what it must have been like in there by the end of the winter, the cows having stood there month after month."

"Just think of the smell," agreed Robin. "I suppose there would have been about 40 cows in those four barns, don't you think?"

"How could they have made the roof with timber as you said?" asked Rona. "I can't see any lying around that you could make a roof with."

"Well," I replied, "it's definite that the houses became bigger and so the roofs higher after the Vikings had been here for a few generations. I think that means that to start with they had to make do with drift-wood; but they soon became organized and began to trade with the ships that sailed between Norway and Iceland. They would have been able to barter ivory, skins, hides and so on for timber. I think that would have been the most important thing that they would need."

"Do you think they had furniture?" asked Rona. "Anything to make it comfortable?"

"Yes, they definitely had tables and chairs, and tablecloths and plates have also been discovered. I have seen spoons and knives in the Copenhagen Museum, but no forks; no one seems to have found any forks. Apparently the Vikings ate twice a day, in the morning and in the evening. One of the sagas tells of a particular king, Harold, who only ate once a day. This must have been unusual or it would not have been mentioned. Apparently this king infuriated everybody because he always insisted on being served first; then, by the time the remainder of the people had had their food dished out, he had eaten enough and so knocked on the table with his knife, which signalled that everything was to be cleared away."

"What did they eat then?" asked Rory.

"Well, I think they lived mostly off the land; their diet consisting of the meat brought back from successful hunts. Of course they would have the fish from the rivers, lakes and sea. Hunting and fishing were their most important activities; although they must sometimes have killed their own cattle and sheep. It is peculiar, though, that the middens which people have dug up contain very few remains of domestic animals, whilst there are lots of bones of reindeer, seals, walrus, a few bears, lots and lots of hares, and even a few big whales, the most common of which was the Right Whale. This is now very rare in Greenland waters, which suggests that the temperature was milder then and the sea temperature higher. The main fish was cod, and, as we know, there is more of those around than anything else."

Robin was digging in the earth beside the ruins. "I think this is one of those middens that you were talking about," he said; "and look what I've found. These bits of bone are definitely bird."

I looked closer and saw that he was right. I knew that they ate grouse and guillemot; and there is a report that whooper swans bred in Greenland up to about a hundred years ago, but not since. Robin now held up a femur of a small mammal.

"I think that is fox," I said, "although they do not seem to have eaten many. There are a few fox skins among the segments of clothing that have been found."

"What did they have all those cows for if they weren't going to eat them?" asked Rory.

"Oh, for the milk," I said definitely, "and also for that sour thin junket that we have eaten in Iceland. They call it 'Skyr', and it keeps for a very long time. They make it by letting the milk go sour, then adding what we would call 'bacterial cultures'. They make more of it by keeping some back and adding a further supply of milk. In fact, it's more like yoghurt than junket, now that I come to think of it. As the milk supply was so important to them, one of their worries would have been how to feed the cows, which was far more difficult than feeding themselves, for cows only ate grass. Just look at the trouble you would have growing a hay field around here."

There was a pile of stones a few yards off, and I realized that it must have been made by clearing the ground in order to leave room for the grass to grow.

"That pile would come in handy when new buildings were being constructed," I pointed out, "and some of them might have helped to weigh down the turf that covered the interlacing rafters of the roofs."

I wondered where, in fact, the Vikings had kept the hay, and stood up and walked over to the back of the byres. Perhaps there had been some sort of barn? We looked around and, sure enough, there was a large oblong building leading off the cow shed. It seemed odd that there was no door to the outside.

"Only one thing for it," I said, "they must have thrown it in from above. They couldn't possibly have carried large quantities of hay through those low doors. But we'll never know because all that muddle in the middle of the building was caused by part of the roof falling in."

According to an Icelandic saga, a cow needed 17·5 kilos of hay a day, and, since cows here would be stalled for 200 days each year, the farmer had to make 2·5 tons per cow annually. That means the cows alone required 50 tons of hay a year, and there was still the goats, sheep, horses and pigs to feed as well. Anyone entering the byre during the winter would be engulfed in the rank smell, for, as we have seen, there was no drain and little air, the stone walls being some ten or more feet wide and lined with turf for protection from the cold. The roof itself was low—a piece of the outer wall-post, found here some years ago, measured less than six feet. There was no "muck out" during the winter, so the cows would practically be standing right under the rafters by spring. The stakes tethering them could be taken out and driven into the wall higher up, as the need arose. But cows in the Middle Ages were small by our standards: six feet from tail to nose.

"How wide are these stalls?" I asked Robin. "Go and measure."

"About three feet wide," he called back, after pacing between the upright slabs of stone.

The most significant ruin was a large oblong with huge, very carefully collected, stones still lying in a regular position on the ground.

"This was the church," I said. "This particular one must have been built towards the end of Erik the Red's life, because the very first church is supposed to be some way off; I wonder where. I read that Erik's wife became a Christian; he would have none of her beliefs and told her that if she wished to build a church she would have do so far away so that it would not annoy him. The story went that she refused to sleep with him, in fact have nothing further to do with him, until Erik became a Christian."

"Let's go and look for it," said Rona, jumping up.

As we walked through the meadow above Erik's farm, it was interesting to consider how Christianity came to this distant land. Apparently, it was Erik's son, Leif, who was responsible for his mother's conversion. He was actually born in Iceland when his parents were living at Haukadal. He must have been about twenty when he led his first long voyage to Norway. Arriving in the late autumn, he went to Trondheim where the king, Olaf, held his court. Leif was apparently popular with the king, who was already a Christian. There is a saga telling that Leif had already read some Christian books, but it seems that he was actually influenced by Olaf for he soon agreed to be baptized. The Vikings tended to rush into things impulsively without thinking them out, so perhaps it was not a carefully considered step on Leif's part. Once he was baptized he forced his crew to follow suit. Leif spent the entire winter at court and was made a knight, or, as the Scandinavians say, a "House Carl". It would have been a great honour for an unsophisticated young man from the rugged northern islands. During the winter Leif heard all about Olaf's attempts to send missionaries to Iceland. They had not had much success. However, when Leif informed the king that he wished to return to his family in Greenland, Olaf seized the opportunity to have Leif take a priest along with him, as well as exhorting the new knight to be sure to "preach the gospel in the west". Leif left in the early summer and it took three months to reach the Greenland fjord of his parents' farm. Erik was not pleased with his son's new ideas and in a saga written about King Olaf, Erik is reported to have said that Leif brought a "hypocrite" to Greenland. Actually it is difficult to translate the word, which means something like "a person who brings misfortune"; but in the context it appears that "hypocrite" was the scathing remark Erik intended. But, as we know, Leif's mother was immediately impressed with the new ideas.

"I can't see any church," cried Rory running ahead of us.

"No," I said, "but remember that we know it was hidden from sight of the house because Erik didn't wish to see it every time he stepped out of his front door."

"What about this?" said Rona, pointing to a horseshoe-shaped round building. "Looks more like a cottage than a church."

"Yes," I said, "but I think it will be it."

This building was eleven feet long by two feet wide, and we could see that it would hold no more than about twenty people standing. The east gable was built of stone, but there was nothing left of the west, which presumably had been constructed with timber. A small circular dyked churchyard surrounded the tiny chapel, in which sixteen graves have been excavated. The bodies were all buried with their heads towards the west. There was very little room for graves inside the dyke, which explains why later the large church was built so much closer to the farm.

I stood in the ruins and imagined what had passed through Erik's wife's mind. It must have been a lonely place for Thjodhild to come by herself. To have given up the great god Odin must have taken a lot of resolution, for the magnificent, dominating, demonic and rather sadistic figure was supreme in the Viking's spiritual hierarchy. He was reputed to have been consumed by his passion for wisdom and for its sake sacrificed an eye and eventually hanged himself. Pitiless and heartless, he was the god of war and of the warriors killed in battle. He, himself, succeeded in battle because he owned a spear, a ring, and an eight-footed horse, all of which had magical properties. Guarded by two wolves, he was brought news from all over the world by two ravens. At night he hunted with his retinue, but his person was only seen by the doomed warriors before whom he would stalk the battlefields: a tall, one-eyed figure clad in a long cape and wearing a broad-brimmed hat. He was credited with knowing men's thoughts, nothing was hidden from him, he knew the "passions of the soul". To achieve his aim of gaining total wisdom, and the knowledge of the mysteries, he stopped at nothing in the way of deceit, cunning and treachery. God of the great ones, an aristocrat and most dangerous of them all, he was sometimes called the "Universal Father"; but the word did not denote any paternal tendencies or sympathy.

If Odin was the god of the great, Thor was the god of the common man. He was far pleasanter and even had a sense of humour. He was a tall, red-bearded, powerful figure who travelled in a goat carriage with a huge hammer, his sign of state. The protector of the Viking peasant he could get the better of all the giants with his mighty hammer. When he raced across the clouds with his team of goats, the thunder rumbled and the lightning flashed. Not very clever, and consequently often outwitted by the giants' tricks, he none the less always won in the end. Quick tempered but easily pacified, the common man understood and appreciated him. He was not merely the subject of stories and tales round the fire at night, but was a truly helpful god who made the crops grow and kept the cows strong. For this reason, and because he was so involved with the people's daily life, he seemed more real and important to them than Odin himself. That is why it was his effigy and not Odin's that stood in the central position in the temples; it was Thor who would be called upon at a wedding to bless the bride with fecundity. Many of the ruined stones were inscribed to him. When Christianity began to creep in and a symbol was needed to resist the potency of the cross, the Vikings chose Thor's hammer rather than Odin's spear, for the latter was too complex, too unapproachable and subtle for the common folk.

There were numerous other gods, each governing a particular human need or action, and Icelandic literature gives a splendid and highly-coloured picture of religious beliefs and customs. Creation and the ultimate end of the world are explained and understood. The belief was that nothing lasted for ever, the gods would eventually fulfil their destiny and then the end of all things would arrive. This belief made room for the emergence of Christianity as a triumphant faith for a newly-born humanity —the Resurrection was something that the early Vikings could understand, which perhaps explains why Thjodhild took to it so readily. The gods demanded sacrifices; the practical farmer's wife would probably be only too pleased to turn to a new belief that did not call for such inroads into the family's limited stock. It was all very well to chop off the head of your horse if you lived in Norway, but a bit hard in Greenland where there was no chance of replacing the farm animals easily.

There is an account of a festival in Norway where the sacrifice involved the slaughter of "nine male animals of every creature". Only this amount of blood would placate the gods. The bodies were hung in a grove near the temple, a sanctuary so holy that each tree was regarded as divine. Sometimes the gods demanded human sacrifice, and then the bodies of the humans would hang alongside those of the dogs and horses. Thjodhild probably decided that in order to protect the settlers against evil powers and the bitter winter weather it was best to bring in more hay than to kill a prize cow.

It was also a great step for Thjodhild to bury her relations in the little church she had had built. The dead were very important to the old Vikings, for they considered that the dead warriors went to a kind of heaven, whilst the women, criminals, outlaws and cowards all went to hell. Everyone had to decide for himself and entrust his fate to a chosen deity. Thjodhild would have had difficulty with her family over burial. Whether the dead went to heaven or hell they still remained with the family whose obligation it was to maintain the grave or burial mound so that the departed would never feel forsaken and therefore obliged to become a ghost. "A walker after death" was terrible and dangerous, and the only course left to the relatives was to break open the grave and kill the ghost a second time. Archaeologists did find that the graves at Thjodhild's church were in fact tampered with, and perhaps this may have been the reason. Apart from Leif, her other children and relations may not have been too convinced of her new beliefs, and would therefore feel obliged to ensure that both Odin and Thor were appeased, as well as the new Christian god. Anyway, some heathens considered the Christian practice of burying their dead in the earth, where maggots would eat up the corpse, a disgusting one; they thought it far better to burn their dead thus enabling the soul to rush off to paradise immediately. But there were so many heathen gods that the Christian one was allowed to "slip in", and the people were prepared to give him a trial. One of the early Viking Christians, St Olaf, is said to have ordered a Viking king, Gaukathori, to adopt Christianity. The king philosophically replied, "If I must believe in a god, it is no worse to believe in your Christ than any other." St Olaf complained that the people were "of very mixed faith". They believed in Christ, but still invoked Thor in matters of seafaring or in dire necessity. The early missionaries must have realized that Christianity would only make progress if it assimilated the earlier superstititions and usages and allowed them to continue under a new guise.

Utter silence. It was easy to imagine and even to feel the bodies beneath my feet. These graves had been for usually tall bodies. It was only the earliest generations of settlers who had been buried here in Thjodhild's church. In one place, however, there was evidence that several people had been buried on top of each other; a sort of mass grave. A feud, an epidemic? There must have been a reason for several people to have died at the same time. Erik's grave is reputed to be here, as well as Thjodhild's and Leif's. There were two other sons, Thorvald and Thorsteinn, and one illegitimate daughter, Freydis. She complicated the relationship by marrying Thorvald. It was these three who, at different times, became involved in the discovery of Vinland and the exploration of North America.

Leif was the first to sail west, with 35 people on his boat, soon after the year 1000. He had wanted his father to accompany him but Erik had fallen off his horse on the way to the shore and sprained his ankle; so he gave up the idea and returned to the farm. Leif's first landing in the New World took place on a flat rocky coast with glaciers which he and his comrades named Halluland. They then steered southwards and arrived at a coast which was flat and wooded. A light nor'easter then blew them across open waters to an island covered with lush grass, after which the wind carried them to the mainland where they headed for a cove from which they towed the ship up river to a lake. They unloaded the ship and constructed temporary houses which they later enlarged as they decided to remain for the winter. Modern investigation has established that the landing place was just above latitude 51 degrees, which, in the Western hemisphere, is at the northern tip of Newfoundland. The information comes from Leif's own log book which also contains descriptions of the grass: "so abundant that there could not possibly be any shortage of feed for the cattle during the winter especially since there was no frost to wither the grass". The distribution of the light and dark hours together with information giving the sun's position when it rose and set on the shortest day are further indications of their landfall.

When Leif returned to Greenland his father was dead and he had to undertake the responsibility for running the settlement. So it was the second son, Thorvald's, turn to voyage westwards. He set out not earlier than 1003 and reached the same site in Newfoundland. But unluckily for him, his party encountered hostile locals. There was a fight and Thorvald was killed by an arrow. His followers gave him a Christian burial and then returned to the Greenland settlement in the spring of 1005. When the third brother, Thorsteinn, resolved to find the land across the sea his intention was to retrieve Thorvald's body, for he had become a devout Christian and believed it very important that the dead should be interred in consecrated ground. He considered Thorvald to be in the clutches of the devil. But the devil got Thorsteinn, too, for he died of an epidemic aboard his ship along with many of his men. Freydis, their half-sister and Thorvald's wife, also desired to see what it was that was tempting and challenging the brothers in this distant land. An opportunity arose when a ship came from Iceland to visit the settlement. Freydis talked the captain into making an expedition to Vinland on a 50/50 basis. They arrived in the new land but an argument soon developed over whether or not they should use Leif's camp site: Freydis maintained that it was hers by right and forced the Icelanders to camp some distance away. With the advent of winter the arguments grew more heated. Freydis stirred up feelings by declaring that two of the leading Icelandic men had taken advantage of her. The two men were killed together with the women in the party; Freydis herself despatching the latter with an axe. The principle of blood vengeance being strong in the Viking world, Freydis's deed led to years of trouble; and, when she arrived back in Greenland, the people so disapproved of her act that they forced her to move across the fjord.

"Come on, Mum," urged Rona, "we've been long enough."

Her plea interrupted my thoughts and brought me back to the present. We walked back to Erik's farm to have another look at the large square building that had been the main church and which, of course, had been built much later than Thjodhild's. Its construction had taken huge quantities of stone; but that posed no problem in this area as the local gneiss split easily into blocks with flat smooth surfaces. The stone was not dressed, but the outer surface of the walls was built with great care and regularity, the stones all matching up. The inner surface was left more or less alone, perhaps to be hung with some sort of tapestry. The church would have stood out in the settlement as it would have been the only building with a naked stone surface; a contrast to the rest which were green with growing turf. Another special feature of the church was its windows. The farm houses had none: the only source of light was the glare from the fire pits and the sparse glow from the blubber oil lamps. The doorway would have let in a little grey daylight and there might have been some kind of outlet for the smoke, although chimneys were unknown: a hole in the roof would have meant a great heat loss, and, with the rain and snow falling on so many days in the year, it seems unlikely that the Vikings would have used this method for ridding themselves of smoke.

Perhaps lack of light explains why so many of their belongings have been found on the sites of the old houses. Leftovers from the meals, such as gnawed bones, cluttered up the floor: the people seemed to have lived among the litter. Everyday pursuits are clearly reflected in the objects that have been found on the floors of the houses, even broken and half-finished tools have been discovered where they had been trodden down, covered in dirt. In one building, the living room stands directly on top of a layer of sheep droppings from an earlier stable; nobody took the trouble to have them removed. Darkness, it seems, covered a multitude of sins! Eskimos, on the other hand, were using carefully cut translucent ice as well as the skin of an unborn seal as windows in their round houses at this time. The Eskimos as well as the environment were against the Vikings.

Sensing something, I looked round: a boy gazed at me; deadpan face, with black hair straight down across inky eyes. I was taken aback, being engrossed with the Vikings. Rory, however, jumped off the wall of the main church and turned a somersault, and the Eskimoid face creased into a jolly grin. The boy rolled on the grass after Rory, the two of them laughing and fooling together. Then I heard hooves and round the corner came a galloping Icelandic pony with two girls clutching each other on its back. It tore past us, mane flying, little hooves kicking up the dry soil. The boy beckoned to Rory and they ran after it. Rona and Robin followed, running after them towards a collection of small shacks gathered around a corrugated-iron building close to the shore.

The Vikings had vanished. The Eskimos on the other hand had already been in Greenland for many hundreds of years before they arrived and are still here now. What was it that made them so successful, I wondered, as I walked through the sunlit grass to the modern village? The Vikings called the Eskimos "the scraelings". There were no Eskimos living in the southern part of Greenland when Erik the Red arrived; as we know he had been particularly attracted to the land because it was empty and he would have been very surprised to know that the country had been occupied since about 3000 BC.

Of course, as I pointed out to the children, the climate at that time was considerably milder and drier than it is today; and small groups of Eskimos migrated whilst hunting across Smith Sound in northern Canada and towards the north-east of the Arctic. The north Greenland coastline differed from its present-day aspect: it is a fact that the sea contained less ice then than it does today, only occasionally are the waters ice-free now. The shores also were less high and steep, which meant that this part was smaller in those distant times; this has been verified by Count Eigil Knuth's archaeological investigations made in the northern district. Count Knuth is the authority on the early settlers and has identified and dated Eskimo tent circles in use as early as 2590 BC. The people lived there for about 1,500 years and their culture, shown by their artefacts and remains, is very similar to that of the Alaskan people living at the same time. Early Eskimo families were always on the move and groups seemed to have travelled continuously, some choosing the north-eastern route while others turned south.

The reindeer first migrated to Greenland, moving slowly down the coast; men followed in their tracks, leaving such clues to their route as fireplaces, charcoal and ashes, cooking stones and middens. The houses had low peat walls, perhaps with stones mixed with the soil, and roofs of skin; each house was heated by a fire. Armed with a bow and arrow the Eskimo hunter lay in wait for the reindeer. To attract the reindeer, which is a very inquisitive though timid animal, the hunters used gulls' wings anchored to a stone to flutter in the wind. The deer would approach the cairn, become frightened and run away directly past the hunter who would be lurking behind a shooting stand constructed of stones.

Hunting on dry land is one thing, hunting the sea is another; and the Eskimo settlers had to find some means of catching seals on the ice or in the tidal openings between the shore and the sea when it was frozen. As their culture advanced, boats, spears and harpoons were found to be more suitable for catching fish and seal than the bow and arrow. The flint points of spears were barbed to catch fish; but then they needed needles and thread with which to construct their boats. Unlike the Norsemen, they had no access to timber, only driftwood washed up by the tide, so they had to use skins. Their culture then, had reached what we would call "stone age" level by the time Erik arrived in Greenland; yet it was a deserted land that met the eyes of the Norse settlers. The Eskimo had left those parts.

Judging from diggings in Eskimo camp sites, a spell of somewhat colder and damper weather set in about AD 500. The permafrost bound the soil again and such conditions made the Eskimos move on. Higher up the midden a layer of peat can be seen with remains of grasses, mosses and small twigs, but otherwise devoid of bones and house refuse. This indicates that towards the end of the period conditions became drier though still cold, the permafrost inhibiting the plant growth. By the Middle Ages the Eskimos found they were unable to cope with the damp cold in their flimsy houses. These were heated by open fires and much fuel was needed; the lack of such fuel may have been the principal reason for their leaving the south. It is extraordinary to think that the Eskimos were far better equipped for coping with extreme cold; that it was in fact the mildness and lushness of the southern pastures that forced them to move on. Eskimo clothes were made of skin, which they left outside the houses and so never thawed. When the owner came out he would put on his dry clothes which of course would then retain the heat and keep him warm. Once skins become damp their ability to retain heat is impaired, as anyone who today wears a sheepskin coat will testify.

Where one group of people find it intolerable to live another will manage to do so. The Scandinavians had been pushed out of their islands by a combination of conditions and had been attracted to this new, vacant land by the very conditions that had forced the Eskimos to move. The first encounter the Vikings had with their predecessors was during Leif's voyage to North America; there he came across several Eskimo settlements on the mainland. His brother, Thorsteinn, also met them when he was camping on the same site. At first relations were friendly although the scraelings were somewhat frightened of the Norsemen. They began to trade with each other but the Eskimos wished to barter their goods for the Viking weapons; Thorsteinn would have none of it. This led to an argument and an open fight during which one of the scraelings was caught red-handed trying to steal a Viking weapon and killed. Real battle then ensued and the scraelings were defeated and forced to flee. At this point the Norsemen decided to leave too, and they set out for Greenland, which of course Thorsteinn never reached. Perhaps this explains why the Norsemen never settled permanently in the new land. It was not until much later that the Vikings encountered the scraelings on their home ground. Then they described them as "swarthy, evil looking men, with wiry hair, having large eyes and broad cheeks". Apparently they did not think the Eskimo a pleasant sight!

I would be more at home among the scraelings than the Vikings, I thought as I hurried after the children and their new-found friends. More Greenlanders were gathered around our canoes. "Kayaks" they were saying in admiration, fingering the canvas and lifting them up to test the weight. The gentle murmuring of their voices was like the sound of the eider duck. There were plenty of dogs about, not huskies however, it being too far south, but genuine sheep dogs. I could see a few scraggy looking sheep as well, but not as many as the Danish government had led me to believe with their accounts of huge sheep stations being run on ranch-like principles as in Australia.

Sure enough, the sheep have hung on longer than the Vikings who first brought them here. To me they looked very much out of their element as they stood around in this landscape of icebergs, glaciers and iceblinks, marking the ice cap at our backs. It was against the Eskimos' nature to herd sheep, so it is surprising that there are any left at all. Dogs and horses, however, are a different matter, they are looked upon as great fun.

The Iceland pony was now galloping in the other direction with three more girls perched on its back, shouting as their long black hair streamed out behind them. Dogs scampered after them, yelping at the pony's hooves. Everyone laughed.

The Greenlanders here, of course, have seen many Europeans

coming to pay homage to Erik the Red, although not many have arrived by canoe! The people moved around us offering Rory biscuits and pieces of dried fish. I sat down among them on the shingle bank. There was a grey light down the fjord, and a wall of ice moving diagonally across the green water. A stiff wind was whipping up the surface and I could see that we would have a hard pull to get back to our camp. A Greenlander offered me a large square lifeboat biscuit. I tried to get my teeth into it, but they made no impression. "This is what to do," said Rona, dunking it for me in the sea. One of the women laughed and leant forward and spread it with honey. This softened the top centimetre and allowed me to munch away at the edge. Some men were busy building a wall, and I realized that they were using the very same method as the Vikings: slabs of turf, then a carefully laid stone sandwiched between more sods. I scrambled to the top and saw this was to be the site for a petrol pump!

"Whatever do they need that for?" asked Rory.

"Their boats," I said, remembering that we had seen no kayaks in this settlement. The whole place was geared to sea travel. Standing up now, I realized that the wind was stronger still. "Come on, come on," I urged, "we must be off."

Too many people helped us lift the canoes into the sea and, when at last we were ready, we were given a great shove which sent us shooting out into the fjord. The sea was really choppy and, as we turned south, the waves slapped into the cockpit. I paddled as fast as I could, but more and more water was sloshing around my legs.

"I'm going to bale," I said to Rory, "make sure you go on paddling."

He took an energetic sweep into the water with one hand but he had pushed the paddle in too deep and it was immediately wrenched from his hand. I had to lean over to retrieve it which meant that we swung into the wind. Sideways on to the waves, the sea was breaking over us constantly. We were nearly over when I just managed to swing us round again. Nothing for it but to keep on paddling despite the icy cold water swilling around my knees. Rory began to cry.

"I'm cold and wet. Let's go in."

This was the last thing we could do. Robin had been much braver and had taken a course farther off shore where it was less rough. I couldn't follow him now and had to put up with creeping along parallel to the coast. The waves got steeper and steeper and I began to wonder whether we would make it at all. On and on, and still we didn't seem to reach the last headland that led to our sheltered bay: it seemed much farther than I remembered. White water was breaking on pink cliffs. Robin and Rona had already rounded the headland so there was nothing for it but to keep going. At last we too rounded it and there was our camp site. The little bay was absolutely calm, the water transparent; it was so tranquil in fact that it was hard to imagine the weather round the corner in the open sea. Already Robin had dumped Rona and was pushing off shore, fishing line at the ready. As we approached him he shouted out,

"Quick, quick, I've caught a monster."

At that moment he dropped his line and we saw an extraordinary sight: the line careering on top of the water, heading in our direction. As it zoomed past I managed to put out the paddle and catch it. It was struggling with such force that the line dug into my fingers but I just managed to take the weight on the paddle when it suddenly went slack. The fish was off.

"Oh, drat you," shouted Robin, cursing me. "It's all your fault. That was going to be the biggest fish ever."

I clambered ashore and then picked out the wailing, soggy Rory. He made his way slowly up to the tent slopping water out at each step.

"Come on," I said to him, "let's have hot tomato soup and cocoa."

Rona was gathering sticks and soon we had the perfect fire around which we all crouched whilst I made the soup. Cooking in conditions like this is very easy. There was no need for complicated preparations and soon we were all swallowing down the thick red soup. Suddenly I screeched as an extraordinary sensation hit my back. I felt heat and stickiness; I put my hand up and withdrew it, it was scarlet. Robin and Rona jumped to their feet.

"What's happened, Mum, what have you done? Are you dying? Must be an arrow."

As I looked at my hand I realized it wasn't blood but soup; I looked accusingly at Rory.

"Well," he said, "it was just too hot and the mug slipped out of my hand. I didn't mean to do it. It was your fault anyway. giving it to me so hot. I think I'll just go home and stay with Granny." He began to cry.

"Leave him alone, Mum," said Robin. "He's just tired."

I stuffed the little boy into the sleeping bag and went back to spend the evening round the fire. Clouds were creeping lower down the cliff on the far side of the fjord. Rain in the night I expect, I thought. It was really dark by 8.30 p.m. and no sign of this "land of the midnight sun". As I sat there I thought about the Norsemen. They must have felt superficially at home as the surroundings were very similar to those in Iceland: the same clear sky lit by the northern light, so different from the atmosphere farther south. But they never really came to terms with the environment. They tried to live the same life they had in Iceland. It was the Eskimos, the scraelings, that were the ones who really belonged here, and, like them, I felt completely at home here too. As we had arrived in our kayaks they had accepted us this afternoon as part of the scene; and I was much happier that we were on their side than on that of the sophisticated, modern Dane, who is, after all, much closer to the Norseman, and equally at loggerheads with the Eskimos, or Greenlanders, of today.

3

THE TENT WAS home to Rory. He hated to relinquish its security, and, whenever I began to pack up, he would snuggle inside the sleeping bag burrowing deeper and deeper, resisting all attempts to prise him out. He was like the slum-dweller who hated to be rehoused away from the environment in which he was safe and confident. The less one has, the more one hangs on to one's surroundings. However, once loaded up and in the canoe, Rory sensed the satisfying feeling of self-sufficiency. We were on our own and needed no support from anyone: no petrol, no shops, no electricity. This was the way to travel.

Before leaving the shore I had to push aside the huge chunks of driftwood which were littering the beach: three trunks from Russia, kegs and barrels, and planks from foreign ships that had foundered, heavens knows where. This was the wood that the Vikings had used for furniture and tools and it had been vitally important to their way of life. Soon we were away, only to meet our second obstacle: the point of hostile slabs which towered above the waves and around which we had to paddle. The waves were breaking against the point and ricocheting back. "Keep out," I shouted to Robin in the other canoe. Icebergs were being driven by the winds towards the shore and piling up at the point. You can paddle close to them, I had told the children previously, for nothing happens quickly with ice and the biggest 'bergs don't roll over; they are too stable. This is quite true of the far north where my previous experience of canoeing in Arctic waters had been. But here, in the balmy south, I had forgotten the effect of the warmer currents and the much hotter sun. Robin and Rona were approaching a large, fat 'berg. Suddenly the water about their canoe surged up. The iceberg seemed to sink then rise out of the sea in a great wall of white; a thunderous noise, then all was hidden in a vast wave. My canoe tipped up and up. Were we going over? I thought so.

But we rode it and I saw the others: a blob of blue on the far side of the now benign looking 'berg. Small chunks of ice were strewn over the water—the only evidence of upheaval.

We went on down the fjord. The ice had been blown close to the shore and we had to keep to the narrow channel—it was far too rough to take the ice on the far side. Kicked up water indicated that there was a bend in the shoreline ahead. Then another huge iceberg appeared in our path. Rona began to shout hysterically that it too would turn over; Robin teased her by going unnecessarily near. As they passed, a small piece of ice fell at the far side causing Rona to paddle like fury for the first time. Robin looked over his shoulder and laughed at me: "See how fast she can go if she wants to."

We rounded a small headland into a quiet bay. A strip of bright green led up to one small house, with a small potato field at one side of it. I had intended stopping in this bay for lunch but Robin, indicating the house, said there would be too many people, and I agreed. I was stiff with sitting in the canoe and would dearly have loved to lie in the grass outstretched but unfortunately it was too crowded, even though it was the only house we had seen since leaving Erik's farm, now a good 30 miles behind us.

"Who lives in it?" asked Rory. There was no sign of life or boat.

"I don't know," I said. "I would imagine that it is a Dane, perhaps married to an Eskimo, who is trying to make a living from sheep farming."

"Yes, yes," shouted Rory, "there they are."

Following his finger I just made out two thin, scrawny-looking, bedraggled sheep far up on the slope above the sea. Not much future there, I thought. No wonder the man appears to have gone away. The potato patch looked well tended though, and I remembered the Danish government's past attitude. They had tried to encourage everyone to live in organized communities with a shop, teacher and visiting doctor. Now they were realizing that this was not such a good scheme; that the people were far more self-sufficient and needed less government back-up if left to themselves in isolation.

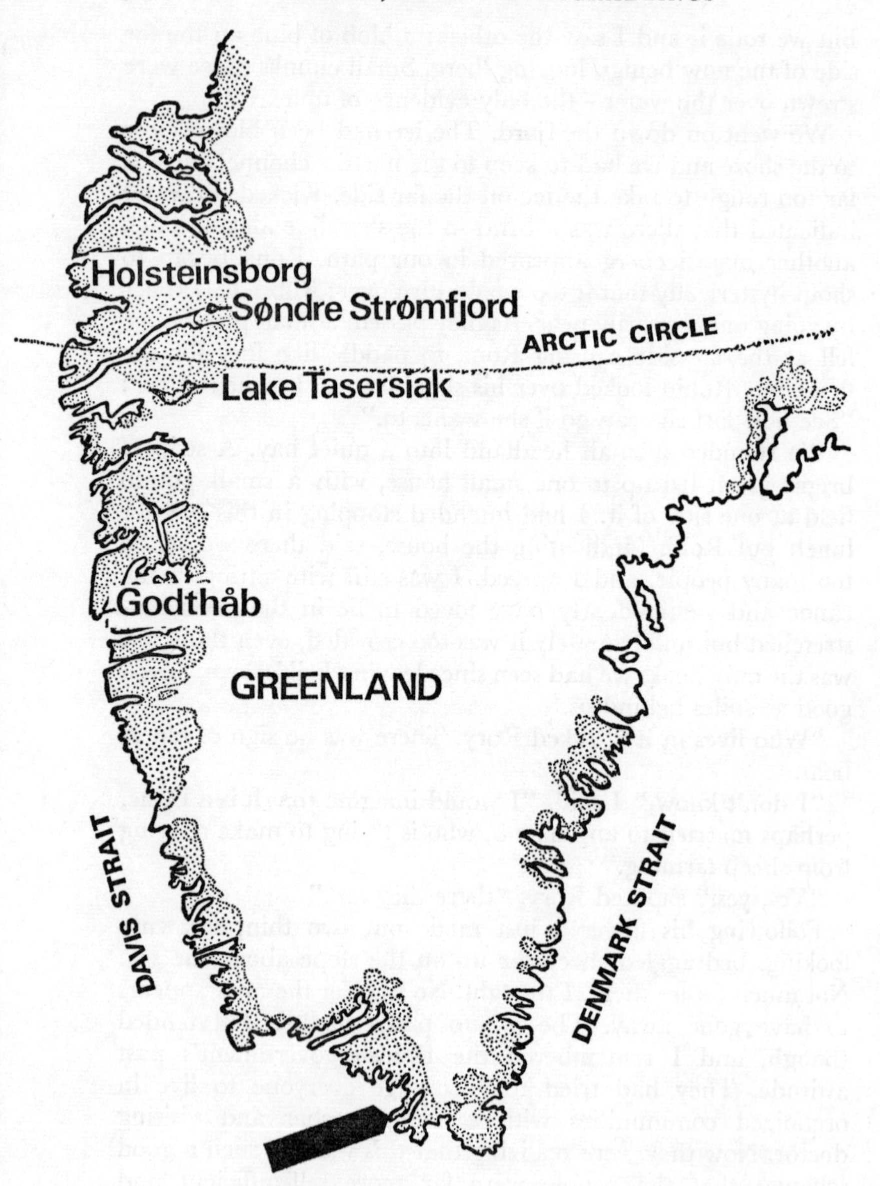
Holsteinsborg
Søndre Strømfjord
ARCTIC CIRCLE
Lake Tasersiak
Godthåb
GREENLAND
DAVIS STRAIT
DENMARK STRAIT

In many cases this realization had come too late; and on the western coast of Greenland one sees deserted settlements, whilst the townships, because of the limited building land, were becoming overcrowded.

I paddled on quickly, wanting to get away from the spot where man had already placed his fingerprint. What is round the corner, I wondered, feeling a sense of adventure again. Adventure is in the mind: it is not risks and desperate situations that make adventures, so much as the "spirit of adventure". Some people have it in greater measure than others; some, of course, do not possess it at all, and they may feel this is the mark of complete maturity. The idea of adventure is now widely accepted in education and I find this strange for it seems to me extraordinary that something which, by its very nature is unpredictable, should come within the province of school at all. As I paddled along behind Robin and Rona I wondered how "adventurous" was the educational idea of adventure. I believe that as soon as one becomes a deliberate purveyor of adventure one loses the spark which is fundamental to the idea. Thus it becomes forced and synthetic, like painting by numbers: a process for people unwilling to take on the agony and ecstasy of original composition. To kill it by technique.

There is a disturbing movement in Britain today that is decaying the spirit of adventure and eroding it. This is being done by the introduction of regulation and certification into such sports as canoeing and mountaineering, sports that have previously enjoyed complete freedom in this respect. The educationalists claim that enthusiasts must prove their competence by attending courses. This "certification" is eagerly seconded by the layman who has no concern for the fact that such a move will have an unfavourable effect on the flair and spontaneity of the sport which, of necessity, is uncertain. Unnecessary activity that involves high risk is always frowned upon by society, yet all agree that "character building" is a good thing, and urge their children to join the scouts, take the Duke of Edinburgh awards, and even encourage attendance at the outward bound-type schools and courses.

But why was I fussing about freedom in adventure? Here in

front of me I had the whole of Greenland. What a privilege. I had no certificate to mark my competence; but I did have many years' experience in living off the land and looking after myself; this, not some hypothetical certificate, gave me the self-confidence to be happy in our present surroundings.

We had a long way to go. I tried to think more deeply as to why I considered it worth while spending my summer sitting stiff and uncomfortable in a canoe, paddling a way through a hostile sea. After all I had been in these self-same waters only the previous summer, but that time in a large ship with all mod cons. Why had I wanted to return? The answer is, that in dealing with oneself, when spending oneself in physical effort, one's spirit experiences a kind of "sonic boom". It calls for faith in things like the climbing-rope, the compass, the fabric of one's canoe, and, of course, in one's companions. And, having faith in these objects and in others leads one to have faith in oneself. But the willingness to step into the unknown, into a new experience, should not be confused with mere recklessness. In foolhardiness there is a certain lack of commitment, one does it "for kicks", for "frivolity", whereas for adventurousness one needs to be completely committed, entirely serious and whole-hearted. It has been said that the true adventurer takes life so seriously that he cannot bear to fritter it away on mere comfort and safety and respectability. It is rather like romance; only true love could turn a long hard slog over the tops of the Cairngorms in Scotland into a real adventure. It is this feeling that is shared by all who love the hills or the sea which is expressed not in words but in physical effort, in competence, and in good companionship.

A sea mist was creeping up.

"Keep paddling," I said to Rory, "I want to look at the map."

I drew it out of my pocket and unfolded the plastic bag in which I had wrapped it. The maps of Greenland have been drawn from aerial photographs; they are, therefore, most accurate when charting the coast line, but fade into vagueness inland. At least we were not navigating by Icelandic spar, I thought. The Vikings used this crystalline, transparent form of chalk to enable them to see the sun through the fogs they so often encountered in the Arctic seas. Farther to the north of Greenland there is less of this thick mist in summer, but here, in the south, it is only too common. It is formed because the land mass is so much colder than the sea in the southern part of the Arctic ocean. Farther north, of course, the temperatures of both sea and land are much the same and the fog doesn't occur.

I remember when we had been on an expedition to reach the North Pole. Our attempt had failed about a hundred miles off shore, and we were faced with returning to the mainland before the summer thaw. We had had clear skies during February, March and April, but then we began to run into banks of mist. It would creep up on us, reminding me of the films I had seen of gas engulfing trenches during the first world war: that evil, intangible substance had crept up on men whose strength and determination were powerless before it. We were in the same position; without visibility we did not know which way to trek. Our compass was useless as we were too far north of the magnetic North Pole, to which the needle points. The danger was that the mist meant open water. It crept up on us from the south whilst we were on the polar pack, and our world began to shrink with every passing minute. We blundered on, picking our way round fingers of ice floes and trying to avoid the open cracks in the ice at our feet. Visibility was practically nil. I began to despair. Ahead of me I sensed the open water whilst on either side of me I felt the pressure of the ice floes on the one hand and the deep drifts of soft snow on the other. Stumbling on, with our sledge mounting ice blocks and careering down ridges of upturned ice floes, we heard gigantic gasps and groans deep beneath the ice; we felt rather like water beetles on a pond. Finally the mist cleared sufficiently for us to see that between us and the mainland was an area of open water. It seemed that the pack of ice on which we were had detached itself from the land mass of northern Canada; and, as far as we could see to the north and south, there was open water stretching to a mile or so wide. We picked our way over the ice to the edge but there seemed no way across the final stretch of water. The opposite shore seemed unapproachable and, without food and paraffin, our prospects looked grim. I thought of Scott and his men dying a mere eleven miles from the depot where ample food and fuel had been cached. However, we did not die: with the eventual lifting of the mist, the sea froze and soon it was strong enough for us to cross to the mainland and return safely home.

Now, in the canoe with Rory, I could see from the map that we had only one camp-site open to us before encountering many miles of steep cliffs looking as if they dropped sheer into the water. After paddling for an hour or two we came towards a low strip of macha which, with a small burn rattling through its middle, led down to the sea. It was protected from the wind by a lush bank of grey willow. The bay in which we found ourselves we immediately christened Stromboli, for there were many large chunks of ice floating around, and one in particular, clear and transparent, was shaped like the volcano. As a shingle beach is lethal to the vulnerable rubberized canvas of our canoes I moored alongside a large boulder, urging Rory to clamber out. One foot on the rock, another in the canoe, he hesitated too long and made the classic movement! Spluttering sea water and shivering he clambered ashore, whilst I stepped out elegantly behind him. The others had also landed and together Robin and I carried the canoes ashore whilst Rona chose a level camp-site. This was easy for the macha was enticing and, sheltered by the willow, it was bathed in hot sunshine.

"I'm going for a swim," announced Robin, pulling off his clothes.

Rory followed him, and soon the two of them were splashing about among the ice. Rona had wandered off up the bank behind the tent, which, by this time, had been pitched.

"Viking ruins here, Mum," she called.

She was right. We could make out the same one-roomed

house with annexes for barns and byres. There was a great feeling of desertion, as if no one had returned since the Vikings departed. Banks of bright blue harebells tossed in the fresh breeze on the lush bank of the midden. Paler blue flowers, field gentians, lifted their faces up to the sun. The scene was a mass of blue, white and green.

"Let's dig," urged Rona, "and see what's underneath."

I had to restrain her, feeling morally bound to leave these ruined sites for the professional archaeologist. It must have been a small family that had lived there, for there was not much land for a large herd of cattle or sheep; and consequently the sons would have had to move elsewhere.

Rory's laughter floated up to us. When did children last play on the sand of this little bay, I wondered, as Rona and I ran to see what the two of them were up to. They were damming the burn.

"I've seen a fish," shouted Robin, "perhaps it's a salmon. I think we might be able to catch it if we move these boulders a bit." I gathered driftwood for a fire and also managed to find some ideal planks for seats, as well as a genuine pot stand. There was plenty to be had for fuel so the billy can was soon bubbling merrily. Whilst the children played in the burn I set about collecting flowers which I then laid in my press to take back to the Herbarium.

The next day was Sunday, 3 August. I awoke at 6 a.m. to the most glorious morning. There was a line of low mist hanging over the water, but the sun was above and it shone right into the tent onto Rory's face. There was no wind. My eye caught a flash of dark blue: a small veronica growing in the pale grass. As I lay in the sleeping bag I could see icebergs gently rolling in the bay, the sparkling water reflecting the sun. Whatever the day might bring, I thought, it is great to be alive at this moment.

By breakfast time it was really hot and as I placed the frying pan on the flames I wondered whether I ought not to use the precious fat on my face, which was creasing from too much sun and wind, rather than use it for the fish. My fingers were rough and sore, too, from the sea water. Too bad, we'll steam the fish, I decided, as I rubbed the lard over my hands and face. After we had finished breakfast and had tidied everything away, I thought it was too lovely to move, so I took off all my clothes and lay naked in the hot sunshine. Thankfully there were no midges. The children were off playing on the boulders as it was low tide, and the only sounds to disturb me were the clinking of the ice in the bay and the tiny stream. Lucky Vikings, I thought, as I munched a bar of fruit-and-nut chocolate. I had intended sharing it all round but instead gobbled it myself. What else could one want? Rona was soon back and came and sat beside me, grasping her knees to her budding breasts, dreaming of boyfriends. I felt so sorry for her growing up and being a girl. Robin and Rory were still tumbling about in the sea, jumping on the boulders, shoving each other, and flexing their muscles in the sun.

"When do you want to go, Mum?" shouted Robin.

"Oh," I answered, "let's wait for the tide to rise, then it won't be such a job."

Another hour went by before I stirred myself to move. I knew we had a long way to go that day and subconsciously was putting it off. But there was nothing for it, we would have to start. The little burn came from a deep split back in the hills, a split that produced the sheer frowning cliff under which we would have to paddle. But when, underway, we approached it in our canoes we found it was not so hostile as we imagined, the angle altogether more gentle than had appeared from the beach. So, in a perfectly calm sea, we had a good day's paddling and the time slipped by. Eventually we found a harbour made of rounded slabs of granite and decided to camp. As we unloaded fish swam around the rudder line.

"Great site, here," called Rory, who had climbed over the slabs to a level site above. When I joined him I saw that we were on a plain: the land was level for many miles. My eye caught the clear blue of a tiny flower: a jewel in the green grass—arctic gentian. I pointed it out to Rory: "Oh, beautiful," he said. Robin came up too and I also pointed it out to him.

The height of his praise was "Oh, lovely" before rushing back to the sea to catch our supper.

"Look at this," he shouted from the sea, "an eel, absolutely camouflaged to match the seaweed."

It was the first I had seen in Arctic waters.

We were tired and put up the tent in record time: the ground being soft it was easy to erect. There was not a breath of wind. The weather looked completely settled and, without a thought, I casually fixed the guy before lighting a driftwood fire alongside. That night the children squabbled as usual as to whose turn it was to sleep next to me; but that resolved, we were soon all sound asleep.

I awoke that night conscious of noise. Wind. It was battering, beating at the tent. I lay and wondered if there was anything to do. I longed for Hugh to be with us, and to be able to go out and check the guy ropes. I lay a bit longer but the tent was flapping, and I realized something would have to be done. There was nothing for it but to crawl out of the warm sleeping bag myself. I pushed open the tent and crept out. The wind tore at my breath; the tent slapped at my face. There was an extraordinary glow in the absolutely clear night sky. A brilliant crescent of moon lit the scene. In the opposite quarter was a fantastically bright planet. Some of the pegs were out. I shoved them in again and hastily crept back into the tent and fought my way between the children for some space. I played ostrich and buried my head under the sleeping bag; but the wind was so intense that I realized I would soon have to go out again. It was warm. I could feel hot air on my face. From inside the tent I could hear Robin's voice shouting at me but could not pick out the words. "What's that?" I screamed at him as I again replaced the pegs and crept back into the tent. I still couldn't make out what he was saying because of the noise from the wind but I could see from his lips that he was asking "It's the *fohn* coming from the west, isn't it?" "Yes." I realized he was right. The noise now made it quite impossible for us to talk. The tent material battered at my back. I sat holding the tent pole, indicating to Robin that he should do the same with the other one. We crouched, using our backs to brace the material against the onslaught of the wind. What on earth should we do? I thought. Take down the tent perhaps and lie on top of it? The wind anaesthetized my mind and made it difficult to think. Much stronger and we would have had it. The tent was not made for this sort of wind. At 3 a.m. it stopped as suddenly as it had begun. Robin and I sank down on top of the sleeping bag. The two younger children had not stirred.

We awoke to absolute calm and it was difficult to visualize the scene of last night.

"Did you hear the wind?" I asked Rona.

"No" she replied, looking at me as if I had been dreaming. "I didn't hear a thing."

Knowing that many miles of steep cliffs were ahead of us I was a little apprehensive. Gingerly we rounded the headland to be confronted by towering columns of basalt rock: the bluff was the steepest we had seen. At the base the rock was pink, a little higher grey, and higher still it turned to black. Farther on we heard the roaring of water and, as we proceeded round a small finger of rock, we were suddenly drenched with spray. A huge waterfall was cascading many hundreds of feet into the sea. I thought I had seen it before and realized that it was similar to the scene at Fjordland in New Zealand where the mountains also rise straight out of the sea. There, also, the rock is too recent to be eroded by streams and they fall off the cliffs straight into the sea.

"I'm going behind it," yelled Robin, and immediately began paddling between the waterfall and the rock; they emerged on the far side, smiling broadly. "Look, Mum, we're absolutely dry."

"Oh, let us go," pleaded Rory; but I wanted to push on. I was terrified that the *fohn* might return before we had found somewhere to camp. My eyes kept sweeping the cliffs ahead, searching for a small gap in the bluffs, where we could pitch a tent. On and on we went. At first it was calm but suddenly the wind again, this time blowing up the fjord. The other two were arguing instead of moving, and I shouted at them urging them forward to the corner I could see coming up. We'll never get round it, I thought, as I felt the wind tug at my paddles every time I raised my arm. Rory was useless. The wind was too strong for him and threatened to blow his paddle right out of his hand every time he raised it above the deck. Still no break in the cliffs ahead. What shall we do? I realized that I was beginning to panic. There was only one thing to do: push on and keep calm. One, two, three, I counted as I struggled against the wind, forcing the paddle down, first on one side and then on the other, trying to make headway. Slowly we inched our way forward, keeping the front of the canoe pointing directly into the wind. At last the cliffs fell back slightly. White water was thrown up into our faces as we changed direction to follow the coastline. Now it was really rough, with the wind onshore hurling the water against the rocks. How could we possibly land without smashing up the boats, I wondered as we pushed ahead. A smooth-backed slab caught my eye. I pointed it out to Robin, who, with a set face was close behind me.

"Get ready," I shouted to Rory. "You'll have to jump as I will not be able to hold the canoe for long."

"Oh Mum," he began to wail, "I can't possibly. I just can't. *You'll* have to do it."

Oh God, I thought, now what are we going to do? But he rallied, and at the right moment nipped out of the canoe and onto the rock, standing upright and holding the canoe as I followed suit. Quickly we hauled in the canoe in time to hold Robin's so that Rona could jump up beside us. Terrified lest the canoe be damaged I stepped into the water; but the rock was smaller than I thought, and I slithered off the end. The waves broke around my shoulders as I grappled with Robin's canoe. I looked at the children: they were laughing, far more amused at Mum having fallen in the water than worried about the weather. The bank was steep and it was difficult to scramble up, but at last we had the two boats perched out of harm's way.

I realized we were standing in a wood, surrounded by willow scrub two or three feet high and very thick and scratchy. Clouds of midges were fastening onto my face. I brushed them out of the way, too tired to make a decision as to where to go next.

"We can't camp here," said Rona.

I pulled up my anorak hood and wandered about, hoping to find a level piece of land in a clearing between the scratchy scrub. There was nowhere. We were in a jungle or level undergrowth, and, what was worse, the wind was battering at me again.

"Not too bad over there, Mum," indicated Robin.

I clambered over towards a large boulder under which was a small gap in the willow, enough to support a tent. The wind tore at the fly sheet as we tried to anchor it.

"Oh," said Robin, "we haven't got the primus. I buried it right in front of the canoe."

I couldn't face going out again, "We'll just have to make do with a cold supper," I said, digging into the bag for the remains of some Ryvita.

There is nothing more tiring or sapping of one's energy than wind, and, when we fell into bed with one last burst of effort, I saw from my watch that it was only 5 p.m. I awoke in the night, squashed and sweaty; the ground was sloping and it was impossible to lie straight. I unzipped the tent before remembering why it had been shut so tightly: a cloud of midges swooped in and immediately began attacking my face.

The morning was quite different. The wind had died and the bay was calm and enticing. Two small islands a few yards off shore beckoned us over. I lay with my head out of the tent and read my Dickens. No midges now; they do not appear until mid-morning. I immersed myself in *Dombey and Son*, so caught up in the emotions of the characters that I could anticipate what each was going to say.

"Let's explore these islands," interrupted Robin an hour later.

"Yes," I agreed. "But, first I want to walk over this rise behind us and see what's on the other side."

"Viking ruins, I expect," said Rona. "They seem to be everywhere. Anywhere there is room for a house, sure enough there's a ruin."

We picked our way over the willow towards some rocks.

"What's this?" said Robin, falling on a piece of old frayed rope. A large iron cage-like contraption was attached to the other end.

"It's a man trap," volunteered Rory as the object clanged shut, spikes rasping together. "It's definitely a man trap. I've seen it on *Blue Peter*."

"For a bear, more likely," I said, looking anxiously over my shoulder. "And it must be Eskimo, not Viking. They never had iron like this. Their traps were made of stone."

"Do you realize that it just missed me?" gasped Robin, white in the face. "I was just about to put my foot in it. Come on, let's get back to the water, it's safer there."

We launched the canoes after having unloaded them, and paddled our way across the glassy water to the islands. Marvellous, ice-smoothed rocks swept down into the sea, and we rounded these into a small lagoon. It was low tide and we swung gently about in the sun watching the fish swimming beneath us.

"Oh come on, let's land," said Rona. "There might be signs of smugglers."

She was the first ashore and was soon sitting on the ground, her head moving from side to side. "Blaeberries," she shouted, "thick with them." We soon joined her.

There is only one way to eat blaeberries and that is at full stretch: we threw ourselves on the ground and ate them straight off the plant. The sun shone down on our backs and the scene reminded me of the South Seas. When I had sated my appetite for the berries I walked away from the lagoon to the height of the island and peered over the top. A sinister sight met my gaze. A vast black wreck was perched on the rocks beneath. Ice was gathered behind it and I could see the current tossing the fjord into a hostile whirlpool reminiscent of the Corrievrecken, the whirlpool north of Jura on the west coast of Argyll. I quickly retreated to the shores of our friendly lagoon. Rona and Rory were playing in the sand as if they were on Margate beach, whilst white slabs had enticed Robin to throw off his clothes and dive straight in. But as soon as I told them of the wreck they were all agog with excitement. As the tide was rising they would not be able to reach it from the shore, however Rona and Robin were determined to try to make it by canoe, thrilled at the prospect of boarding the rusty metal hulk. I didn't want to go, it looked hostile and evil to me, so Rory and I remained behind.

Where had it come from? I pondered as I sat on a promontory and watched the two of them paddling their canoe along the shore. I knew the boat was not Viking, it dated obviously from the last war and was probably part of a convoy crossing the North Atlantic; such convoys often had to seek shelter in the Greenland fjords. Too large for such narrow waters, this ship had escaped a German torpedo to be destroyed by more elemental enemies: current, ice, tide and wind; these had combined to destroy the modern merchant vessel. What chance had the Vikings then, in their small open boats with no engines?

It was not until 1887 that the first steam vessel came to Greenland waters. This was the *White Bear*, a Danish-built, three-masted barque with a 300 hp engine, reinforced for navigation in ice. In those days that amounted to an iron-sheathed bow and an extra layer of hardboard. For eight years she continued her voyaging until she ran aground. The passengers and crew managed to scramble to safety on to a convenient rocky lee where they found shelter in a cave; their escape was only just in time for the vessel virtually broke up under their feet. They were not the first to seek shelter on that rock, for they found a sinister message scratched on its surface: "Eighteen sailors died here and me next." But the *White Bear*'s survivors were saved; not so those aboard the whaler, *Carstower*, brought in to replace the *White Bear*: she disappeared without trace, taking with her 29 souls, some of whom had survived the *White Bear*. Nansen, the Norwegian explorer, had to beat the ice in order to carry out his intention of drifting across the Polar Sea; and his ship, the *Fram*, influenced the design of Greenland coast steamers for many years thereafter. The next type of ship to appear in these waters was a strange looking craft. Rigged as a three-masted, top sail schooner, it sported a tall, narrow chimney that stood forward

Discovered grave: Viking or Scraeling?

Eric's fjord

Rory Simpson map-reading

Bones lying in Eric the Red's byre: Eric's fjord

Robin and Rona at the waterfall, Eric the Red's fjord

Scraeling in kayak, Narssaq

Eskimo eating boiled seal meat, Narssaq

Hvalsey church, the site of the famous last wedding; Myrtle, Rory and Robin Simpson in canoe

Hvalsey church: Rona

Viking ruins near Hvalsey

Myrtle, Robin and Rory at Igaliko fjord

of the superstructure, rather as an afterthought. The superstructure itself was high in order to accord greater visibility of the ice ahead.

The only regular vessels in these waters belonged to the Greenland Trading Company, and their first steel vessel was the *Hans Egedy*, a three-masted schooner. It was the first serious attempt at a rational design for both passenger and cargo ship in ice-filled waters. Tubby shaped, she had a double bottom, tanks for the transport of whale oil in bulk, a two-bladed propeller, and was capable of speeding up to ten knots. Because of her shape she was tossed about in the north Atlantic waters, much to the disturbance of the stomachs of the 24 passengers she had been equipped to carry. At the outbreak of world war one, the pride of the Greenland Trade Department fleet was the *Gertrude Russ*. Many ships setting out into the ice during that war were never heard of again, but the *Gertrude Russ* survived. She stayed afloat until February 1942 when, during the second world war, whilst on convoy to New York, she ran aground off Newfoundland and was a total loss. Before the month of February was out the *Hans Egedy* had also been lost, probably in the Baffin area. As soon as the war ended the Trade Department commissioned new ships for the Greenland service. The first was made of wood and was the largest motor ship built this century. She was undeniably the most curious of the many strange ships that had sailed the Greenland route. The wood for her construction had been hoarded throughout the long years of the war and, built when the skills required for building ships with wood no longer existed, she was considered truly amazing with her egg-shaped hull and diesel-electric engine. But she had a short life for she was soon consumed by fire. However, the Greenland Trade Department were in the process of building another ship, the *Hans Hedtoft*, and this proved to be the world's most advanced Arctic vessel. At the end of January 1959 the ship left Denmark on its maiden voyage to south Greenland and back to Denmark. The captain, who declared that he "most definitely had the world's best Arctic ship", reckoned that he would beat all previous records across the North Atlantic. He was warned, however, that there was a great deal of snow around Cape Farewell, and was advised that he should pass farther south, and not keep close to the coast. On 30 January at 17.45 hours, the ship hit an iceberg 27 nautical miles south-east of Cape Farewell in a blinding snowstorm. The ship, which had a gaping hole in the engine room which soon filled with water, stopping the engine and other vital equipment, was soon in grave distress, drifting helplessly in the high wind. The distress signal, "Have hit iceberg. Water in engine room rising fast. Assistance necessary", was first picked up by a German trawler which hurried to the area, keeping in close contact with the *Hans Hedtoft.* In all they were in contact fifteen times but, just as she reached the reported position, the trawler received a further message: "Am sinking slowly. Urgent assistance needed." There were two further signals and then complete silence. The trawler searched the area, but her efforts were marred by the 30 feet waves and the floating ice: she narrowly avoiding hitting an iceberg herself. She could find no trace of the injured vessel. Icelandic, American, Canadian and Danish planes hurried to the area and began a systematic search but they too could find no trace of the *Hans Hedtoft.* A few weeks later a single lifebuoy from the vessel was washed ashore on to the coast of Iceland: it was the only thing ever recovered from the ship which had sunk with the loss of 95 passengers and crew. Ironically, among the passengers had been a member of parliament from Greenland, who, two years earlier, had warned that winter passenger voyages were incredibly dangerous. His warning had gone unheeded. However, since the loss of the *Hans Hedtoft*, all passenger voyages between Greenland and Denmark have been prohibited during the period from December to March.

The sea route to Greenland from Denmark was the thin life-line that connected the northern colony with the motherland. Without it, the Europeans had insufficient means of existence, for, if the ships carrying the provisions and equipment necessary to sustain life failed to arrive, then the situation became well-nigh impossible. As those first followers of Erik the Red found, the waters around Greenland are some of the most hazardous in the world, and many ships foundered during the long voyage, as the Danish records of the numerous maritime enquiries that followed successive shipwrecks confirm. One such enquiry concerned the frigate *Maria Louisa*. She weighed anchor at Copenhagen on 14 June 1800, but became wind bound at Elsinore where she remained until 21 June. The following day she sighted the coast of Norway but then had to ride out a gale, during which it is recorded that one of her sailors died of scurvy. On 7 July she encountered a fresh storm off the Fair Isle; and by September many of the crew had to be relieved of duty owing to scurvy and rheumatism. On 14 September the captain, who was so weak that he could not write, relinquished his command to the first officer; by the end of the month both the captain and the second officer were dead. By this time the coast of Greenland had been sighted but fog and snow prevented them from reaching it. On 4 October it is recorded that the ship was drifting helplessly north as there was no one to reef the sails. Another storm blew up on 11 October but the following day the surviving crew were able to drop anchor within sight of land. Three men, who were still able to row, went ashore to find some Eskimos; they returned to the vessel completely exhausted on 15 October. Yet another storm hit the ship whilst at anchor and she was driven on to a rock where she keeled over to port and lost her wheel. All masts were cut away but this failed to save her. The remaining crew launched the lifeboats and, on their last legs, rowed to the nearby town of Gotharb on the west coast. No one went on those early boats for pleasure!

There is yet another account in the archives, this time of a voyage made in 1863, by a passenger, or "embarker" as he would be known then, on the brig *Tjalfe*. His cabin, which was in the aft hold, was five feet long by eight feet wide and separated from the rest of the hold by a few stinking boards. This he had to share with another passenger. The entrance to the cabin, which he called "the lobster pot", was the aft hatchway, and was closed as soon as they had gone below. There being no room for bunks both men had to sleep on the floor. In bad weather he had to spend all his time in the cabin to avoid the dangers and soaking of being on deck. Far worse than the cramped quarters, however, was the smell of the ship, which, coupled with the pitching and tossing—worse in his cabin because of its proximity to the hold—and the filthy black sludge that covered all, made conditions well nigh unbearable.

Back now to the present. By this time Robin and Rona had reached the hulk. From where I was sitting I could see them searching for a place where they could scramble up the sides. Their frail canvas canoe looked vulnerable and naked against the rusted jagged metal of the wreck: to me the man-made vessel seemed far more evil and hostile than the wind and tide. Suddenly they were back in their canoe and paddling away: something had frightened them. "What's up?" I shouted as soon as they were within hailing distance.

"We saw an eel," replied Rona. "It was huge, absolutely enormous. I couldn't bear to look at it. It seemed to be living on the wreck. Robin said it would have eaten all the dead bodies, and that is what made it so big. It was as thick as your legs, Mum; absolutely fantastic."

They shot back to the lagoon with white faces.

The tide was now rising and therefore it was possible to canoe over the sand spit joining the two islands. This brought us to the far side where rounded, ice-worn slabs swept straight into the sea, which, at that point, looked incredibly deep. The map marked it as 283 fathoms. How ironic that the ship had run aground so close to this deep water. Above the slabs the ground was black with berries, and I wondered if this might be the origin of the Viking name for Vinland. Were these the berries that they found when they reached the new land? Some we saw that day were as thick as peas and, crushed, they would ferment well into wine.

It was lovely to slip through the water round the island rocks with their ledges of lush green.

"Look at that beach," shouted Rona, "best yet."

It was on the mainland, a little bay of sand. It was a stiff pull across to it with the rising tide rushing up the fjord, but we made it and jumped ashore. The children could not resist the sand: Rona and Rory jumped and rolled in it, gambolling about, burying each other, tossing the sand into the air, loving the feel of it through their toes. Robin and I left them there whilst we trudged back up the coast to collect our gear. The water was lapping gently against the slabs that had given me so much trouble when making a landfall the previous evening; I was glad to leave that site with its sinister associations of wreck and man-trap.

The light was low when we returned to the others who were still playing on the sand.

"Look what I've caught," yelled Rory as we came up.

It was a Daddy-Longlegs.

"How does it keep its legs warm? he asked. I had to admit that I did not know.

Ravens were circling above us beside the towering cliffs, squawking bad temperedly at each other.

"Tomorrow should see us into Illua," I said, pointing at the map. We could see that the cliffs gave way to a great finger of sea which thrust three or four miles inland merging into a narrow spit that formed the upper part of a lake. The highest mountain in the locality rose up on the far side of this stretch of water. I pointed to it on the map.

"I want to climb that," I said to the others. "We'll camp at the bottom of it tomorrow and have a go the following day."

4

"ANOTHER INCH AND the guy ropes will be in the water."

"Oh, don't fuss," I retorted to Robin, "the tide can't possibly come in any further. Grass just doesn't grow under the sea."

Relentlessly, however, the water continued to rise; but I was so tired that I preferred to be a Canute than move from my position.

We had left very early that morning on a low tide, but it had been a stiff paddle, particularly as we edged out past the wreck on the other side of the small island. As we pushed on we kept rounding point after point, they seemed to be never-ending. Before we had gone far the wind had increased and the tide had changed and the continuing cliffs offered no chance of a landing place. Finally, after struggling for what seemed an age, we rounded the last point and found ourselves in Illua, paddling up the narrow finger of sea which reached back into the hills.

When we saw a flat piece of shore we headed for it. It looked marshy, and, sure enough, when I stepped ashore water oozed between my toes. To one side it seemed a little drier, becoming a stretch of turf-like macha.

"Look at the fresh seaweed, Mum," said Robin. "We can't camp here."

I looked around but there didn't seem to be anywhere else.

"Oh, I'm sure the tide doesn't often come above this grass. Once in a blue moon," I said.

"Well, I hope you're right," he replied. "The tide is still coming in, you know, and it has a long way to go. It is not yet four o'clock and high tide is not until six, I think."

"Why are all those dead fish about?" interrupted Rory, scuffing up large backbones, heads and tails.

I looked at them closely and realized that they were not cod.

Salmon, I wondered, remembering the significance of the fresh-water lake beyond the spit which we could see from here.

"We'll go and catch some in the morning," I told them. "I'm far too tired now."

We had our supper and then crawled into our sleeping bag. How high will the water come? I wondered. I lay and watched the tide rise to the level of my eye; it seemed to get higher. Then pieces of charred wood floated across my vision: our fire! I raised my head and saw that the water was actually flowing across the site of our fireplace.

"Come on, Mum, I can't stand it any more," announced Robin. "Don't be daft, we've just got to move."

Of course he was right.

Too late, we began to scramble about collecting our belongings. Anything lying outside the tent was already wet. There was nowhere to go. The land rose steeply behind us whilst on all sides the bank fell straight down to the water. There was nothing for it but to try higher up and to drag the tent up with us.

"Have you ever had a tent with a seat inside, Mum?" asked Rona indicating the varying levels of the ground on which we had tried to pitch it finally. I cursed her for being cheeky.

"Oh," said Rory, championing his sister, "you should like your only daughter, Mum."

"There is nothing wrong with this site," I said stonily, and wriggling into a sleeping bag which could only occupy one third of its normal space.

"We're still not safe, you know," pointed out Robin. "The tide has already completely covered the lower camp site."

I had a fitful night's sleep, waking continually to check the level of the water. When at last it began to fall I found I could not get back to sleep for we were all piled into one corner. However, I must have dropped off for I awoke to brilliant sunshine and complete calm. In front of us the water seemed to occupy an enormous expanse which, being still and placid, resembled a Chinese painting. I lay basking in the sun's rays allowing the silence to enfold me.

"Make pancakes for breakfast," interrupted Rory.

"Okay," I said reluctantly, "but you'll need to go and collect some wood. The tide washed it all away."

He and the others moved off slowly collecting dead twigs among the willow trees above the tent, whilst I mixed flour with water and emptied our last bit of dried egg. Soon we had the pancakes sizzling in the pan.

"More, more," cried Rory.

"No, this one's mine," complained Robin, "You've already had seven."

I scraped the last of the batter into the pan, and it rose into a leathery slab about half an inch deep which, at home, would have been considered disgusting, but, here, delectable.

"There're some ruins up there," pointed Robin, mumbling through a mouth full of pancake. "There are some big flat stones, as if they were graves. They're so big that they must have had metal crowbars to move them."

"Oh, show me," cried Rory. "I must have a look."

The rising ground behind the tent was a herb slope; a plant community growing on a sloping mountain meadow. Near the water, because of the willows, the predominant colour was grey, but here, with the mountain alder, which only grows between the 61st and 66th latitudes, as it needs the shelter of the southern fjords, there were dashes of darker green. As we gained height, the ground was tinged with red and yellow, and, looking closely at the ground round my feet, I realized that we were surrounded by multitudes of differing plant species; a contrast to the rocky scree slopes we could see on either side of us. Most of the plants had soft, juicy, light-green leaves, that formed a rosette close to the ground. An orchid! I could just pick out its small white stem of flowers with the dark green leaves and the scent of lily of the valley. There are five different orchids in Greenland: this was the "butterfly". The red that I had noticed was the rose-bay willow-herb, at its best now, in early August.

"That's the flower we used to eat at Igdlorsuit," said Rory, stuffing some petals into his mouth.

I remember that it had tasted of honey.

Ferns were growing among the knot grass, and the tall plant was the angelica.

"Why do you think so many different plants grow here?" asked Rona. "There must be at least 50."

"Well," I replied, "this slope must be exactly suitable. That means it must lie in a position to catch all the snow in winter, as these soft, juicy leaves need an ample cover to insulate them against the low temperatures and to prevent their delicate shoots from drying up. Then, in the spring, the melted snow will provide water just when it is most needed by the germinating seeds; and, being on a slope, it will drain quickly to allow the plants a long growing time. The plants need all the sun that they can get so the snow must be gone by May. The lushness of the growth will also have something to do with those rocks above. You can see from the different colours in the rocks that they contain various crystals and minerals which would be washed off by the water into the soil on the slope. The lushest places are usually to be found on mountain slopes. But it takes only a slight decrease in the amount of water in summer to change the whole composition of the herb slope; and that is probably what happened in Viking times. A rise in the temperature of a few degrees would certainly dry out the slopes and alter the entire situation. What the Vikings needed were plenty of slopes like these, facing south beneath vertical cliffs thus giving a constant dripping and seeping of water from the melting snow above and day-long sunshine to enable the plants to grow during the summer months, not forgetting, of course, a thick blanket of snow to protect them in winter. Just look at these plants. There are more here than would grow in the same situation at home on the west coast of Scotland."

By now we had reached a level place, and, as Robin had indicated, there seemed plenty of evidence of Viking occupation. He took us immediately to one of his graves: a big, flat slab lying flush with the ground.

"Help me lift it," he said kneeling down beside it and trying to prise it up.

"Just a chink then," I replied.

We wedged in a small sharp stone, and then another, until

some light shone in. We looked straight on to a Viking skull! I was immediately sure it was Viking because of the shape of the head. Eskimos are Mongolian, a round-headed race; and this skull was not. I quickly looked away: what an intrusion of the modern world!

"How long has he been there? queried Rona.

Looking at the ruins, I could see that this had been a more recent dwelling than that of Erik the Red's.

"Only about 700 years," I replied.

Like Erik's farm this front door commanded a magnificent view across the fjord. Entry into the house was made along a flag-stone paved passage with the fireplace opposite the entrance, well protected from the draught. There were signs of a cooking pit, for pieces of charred bone and charcoal were mixed with the ashes. As the children moved the large boulders, I could see that the floor of the building had been of stamped gravel; and I could also see pieces of unburnt bone, probably a seal, lying around. I tried to imagine the scene with the roof intact. The people would be crowded together under the sloping ceiling, which was supported by uprights along the inner wall; their flushed faces lit by the glow of the great fire, the smoke from which, when the wind beat it down through the gaps in the turf roof, would smart their eyes and make them water. An open drain would run along one side of the room through which the water would flow; very convenient for cooking, I thought. (We never seemed to camp so close to fresh water, and I was continually imploring Rory to fill the billy can.) The drain had been widened at one corner, making a kind of basin to serve as a reservoir. The Vikings were, of course, forced into this method of retaining water as there were very few grounded springs in Greenland owing to the thin strata of soil. In Scandinavia they could probably have dug a well. Erik the Red had been lucky at his site, for there had been a spring close at hand. More rooms opened up off the main room which indicated that many people had lived on this farm and in a more sophisticated manner than the earlier settlers.

This made me think again about the graves: these people would have been Christians. In heathen times the Vikings would have been buried with all their goods and chattels: objects that had been useful in the past and would be useful in the new life. A man's wife would also be buried with him, and, if they so wished, his slave women as well. These women looked upon it as a great privilege and, whilst other slaves were preparing the body, cutting the clothes and laying out his belongings, the doomed women would drink and sing, as though awaiting a happy event. When the moment came the women would be placed alongside their master, then the door of the grave sealed or the flag stone laid in position; the women of course would then die as well. The coming of Christianity put a stop to this practice. But it did not stop their method of population control. When a new child was born, the family would carefully consider whether or not there was enough food to cater for another mouth. If not, the child would be carried outside, carefully laid between upright stones where, with a flagstone laid across the uprights and a piece of fat in the baby's mouth, it would be left to die of the cold.

"Look Mum," shouted Rona from outside. "Do you think this is one of those baby-killing places?"

I stepped over a low wall and walked to where she was crouching down beside just such a place as I had been thinking of. There were the flagstones forming a tiny coffin; the bones had been scattered long ago.

"Why did they do it? Why?" cried Rona. "How could they be so cruel? Think of the little babies dying here, screaming for food. How do you know they did it, anyhow?"

"Well," I tried to explain, "experts have found very few infant skeletons in the graves, which, since infant mortality was very high in the Middle Ages, is surprising. People died from all kinds of diseases and, in Britain for instance, if you had five children in those times you would only expect one to grow up. So our churchyards from about the year 1000 were full of children's bodies. That there is none here seems to be explained by the fact that so few children were allowed to grow up. It is known that the Norsemen practised this harsh form of family control from their sagas, and one of them, the *Finn Boga Saga*, describes how a child is placed between the stones with a piece of suet in his mouth to stop him crying and another stone on top sealing him in. They would rather do this than see the child grow up and not have enough food to feed him with. We can see, even now, what a marginal existence the farmers around here must have had. There was nothing to spare and the situation was worsening all the time. If we were to dig up that body over there, I am sure we would find it bent and wizened from privation. The early Vikings, Erik the Red's men, were over six feet tall, and the women well over five feet: that was why they called the squat Eskimos 'scraelings' or 'small men'. Those early graves show they were in first-class health with excellent teeth; whereas the later Viking graves indicate that a deterioration had set in, for, when they died, the later Vikings were twisted with arthritis and their bones showed that they had suffered from all kinds of vitamin deficiencies. It seems that some were so bent that when they died they could not be straightened out before being placed in the grave. And that too is described in one of the early sagas."

Robin interrupted me. "Look at the tide," he shouted.

Heavens, it was rising.

"Highest yet. Come on, Mum. We'll need to shift the tent again," he commanded.

"Okay, okay," I said, "I'll be down in a minute. I want to have a look at those round stones over there. I think it might be an old Eskimo house."

"Don't be daft, Mum," Robin remonstrated. "That's our woodpile floating away now. I can see the groundsheet is awash. Come on."

Nothing for it but to give in, and I ran down the slope after Robin. We lugged the tent higher still.

"This time it has got a sleeping shelf," said Rona, "exactly like the Eskimo house. Remember?"

Rona was right. "Well, you and Robin will have to be anchor men in the sleeping bag, and hold Rory and me on."

"There are Eskimo sites everywhere," said Robin. "I can tell by the large stones that they used to hold down their tent canvas; but I don't know whether they are old or new."

I walked along the edge of the shore to the spit, and, as

Robin had said, there were dozens and dozens of round tent circles. Likewise I did not know how old they were, for a modern Eskimo, when travelling, still uses the same method his ancestors used to tether his tent. There were fish heads everywhere and I suspected that the Eskimos, or Greenlanders, still came to this place when the salmon were on the run. We were obviously too early for this, for Robin fished and fished but only managed to catch cod for our supper that night.

My sleep was constantly interrupted as I kept falling off the sleeping shelf. The same applied to the others and eventually we decided to abandon it and managed as best we could on what remained of the floor. I lay awake and planned what I wanted to do the following day. Climb that mountain that rose behind us. At six we were all fully awake and ready to depart by half-past. Our feet felt rather cramped in our climbing boots after weeks of wearing soggy gym shoes. We set off up the sloping meadow, through the wintergreen and orchids, the knee-high buttercups and the grey-green willow scrub. As we gained height the growth grew sparser and sparser, although we noticed some pink splashes on the grey stone.

"Look at this," said Rory, pulling at my hand to indicate the yellow and green markings of sulphur. "And this, and this." He had by now picked up at least five stones.

"For goodness sake, put those down", I said. "You'll be able to pick them on the way down the mountain. No one carries stones like that when trekking up a mountain at the beginning of the day."

The vegetation ran out and we were now ascending steep scree which eventually gave way to smooth slabs. Scrambling over these we breasted the col which gave us a view of an inner corrie. Steep walls of scree rose on all sides and our view to the front was masked by a miniature Table Mountain.

"Where's the summit?" asked Robin.

"I don't know," I answered. "I think we will have to go to the back of this corrie and round that spur. That should surely lead to the ridge that will give us access to our mountain itself."

We started off on a horizontal traverse. Robin was ahead.

"Come on," I shouted to Rory. "Hurry up, we mustn't get left behind like this."

It now became necessary to use our hands to maintain balance. Rory and I rounded a finger of rock to find Robin standing with Rona gazing down at their feet. They were perched on the brink of a horizontal chimney.

"It's a witches' leap," I said, thinking it to be exactly like Killicrankie, where the highlanders leaped the river but the English redcoats, unable to follow suit, all fell in. "Well," I said looking round, "thank Heavens we don't have to try and jump it. I can see where we can round it at the top."

We were forced to make a detour of a good quarter of a mile before we could round this great gap, or fissure, in the rock. after that the going was easier and soon we were standing on the floor of the corrie with the back wall rearing above us. Only then did I turn to view our fjord and beyond it to Igaliko Fjord and the open sea. What a thrill. The water seemed grey with chunks of ice merging to a pale sky. We toiled on. Our only way was to ascend the steep scree slope into the higher corrie. Robin took up the pace, pursued by Rona; I followed with Rory. The mountain did seem nearer but, as we gained more height, my heart sank as I could see that the final arête ran out into a steep face of rock.

"Oh," wailed Rory behind me, "this is the worst day of my life."

Robin and Rona waited for us to catch up, and, at that point, I was all for going no further. Robin's enthusiasm, however, spurred me on and soon he was approaching the bottom of a steep snow chimney. He kicked a ladder of steps with the toes of his boots and gained height fast; it seemed to me that he was heading through unclimbable slabs. I knew there was no point in me yelling advice to him; he had to find out for himself. Sure enough he was soon forced back to the scree. Rona, above us, with good balance was scrambling on, sending a few small stones down to myself and Rory, who, by this time, was going slower than ever. Robin started up again and we followed, up and up, up and up, sending a cascade of boulders and pebbles down to the corrie floor. We reached a traverse and ahead or me I could hear Robin shouting and see him waving his arms about. Finally, with me pulling a reluctant Rory along by the hand, we joined the two of them. What a view. There ahead of us was the ice cap where in greys and whites it joined the sea; and directly below us was a glacier. We were perched on a narrow arête flanked by a wall which was at least a thousand feet high. There was no doubt about it: this was the end of the way for us. The summit, above the wall of rock, was unobtainable. But before turning back I drank in the scene before and below me. The ice cap licked round far to the west and, turning slightly, I could see the entire map of the southern fjords of Greenland at our feet, with the sea edging its way into the grey rocks.

"What a daft place to live," said Rona. "Why on earth did the Vikings think that they could settle and farm here?"

Sure enough the land looked completely inhospitable from this point; man seemed to have no place in this world of rock and ice.

"We mustn't waste much time," interrupted Robin, pointing to the glacier from which the cumulus grey clouds were boiling up.

"You're right," I said. "There is bad weather coming."

I realized we would have to hurry; we had waited too long as it was.

"We could call this Everest," said Rory. "If we had to get to the top of this mountain I would not have to do anything more for the rest of my life."

"Lucky for you that we didn't manage it then," I said. "Come on, we must be off."

I was dreading the descent but once we were on the small scree it was fairly easy and soon we were at the edge of the snow.

"Be careful, be careful," I shouted. "Wait for me." But it was too late. The kids were off, they were already descending. Robin was first, glissading easily down with his weight on the heels of his boots. He turned and twisted as if vedeling, as though he were descending the best alpine downhill piste. All the children were good at this, even Rory; with short turns he whizzed down in a way that I could never master. I had to carefully kick steps, one foot below the other, and with no ice axe, I had to watch that I didn't slip. Down and down and down. At last we stepped off the snow on to the corrie floor, much to my relief. Now the rocks and then the slabs. At the witches' leap we stopped. A flash of colour was darting among the rocks: a butterfly. The Greenland Tortoiseshell. What on earth was it doing here? It was at least 4,000 feet high in the rain.

Rona and Rory were as tired as I was. We were now dragging one foot in front of the other. Back and back. When we came to the first vegetation we found blaeberries. Rona and Rory flung themselves on them and soon gobbled them up.

"Better ones down here," shouted Robin some way ahead of us. They ran towards him, their tiredness forgotten in their enthusiasm for the mouthfuls of refreshing juice. "Best yet," yelled Robin still further ahead. With the lure of berries I would be able to walk Rory any distance, I thought. The mere mention of berries and he would be off.

It was easy to see where the Vikings had found their slabs for their buildings and graves. Huge chunks of rock had split from the mountain in the winter frost. I peered carefully; my ambition in life was to find a runic stone. Nothing here though. Wait, was that a man-made scribble on the rock? I looked closer and clambered into the crack between two large slices of rock. As I looked down my eye caught something white below me. I could only just get my shoulder in but no more. Nothing for it but to extract myself and yell for help.

"Rory," I shouted, "I've found a treasure." He was reluctant to leave his berries but he did come at last. "See what's down there," I requested. "I believe it might be something belonging to the Vikings. Try and get it."

He wriggled back the way I had but soon began to squawk. "My head's stuck," was his muffled cry. Of course our heads were the same size and he would be able to go no further than I. He extricated himself whilst I searched for some implement with which to extract my find. There was nothing. So I pushed and shoved my shoulder deeper into the crack, edging my arm downwards, my fingers picking their way hungrily towards the object. Finally they closed round something smooth and, very carefully, I drew it out, securing my hold the nearer it came to me. I was clutching a long, carved wooden ladle which had become white with age.

"Viking or Eskimo?" asked Rory at once, uttering my own thought. Was this a priceless Viking artefact or a relatively recent Eskimo loss?

It was raining down here by now, so we hurried to the tent. Suddenly there was a fluttering at my feet: a ptarmigan. It indignantly squawked at me for disturbing its peace; and I was as much surprised as the bird. Looking flustered and considerably put out, it glowered at us from the boulder upon which it had taken refuge: the red blotch over its beak the only break in its camouflage.

"Do you see it?" I asked Rory.

"Yes, of course," he answered. "That's nothing. I've seen plenty of them at home."

I was cross with him for taking this attitude. "I, too, have seen dozens of them before, but I am just as excited to see one here in Greenland."

"I've seen dozens of robins before, too," he said pointing to some small birds fluttering among the seeds of the willow behind us.

"Well, you're wrong there," I pointed out, "for those are red pols, and I've only seen them once before, in Scotland. Look carefully at their beaks. Do you see? They're finch-like, like snow buntings, fat and squat for picking up seeds. I think these are my most favourite Arctic bird. Do you see how they flutter around in a gang?"

I crouched down to look more closely at this little bird. There is a type of red pol that is only found in Greenland. To be sure it is a close cousin of our hoary red pol which is often to be seen on the west coast of Scotland; but this particular species has been resident in Greenland since the period of glaciation, when it was isolated from the rest of the world. It has therefore developed the ability to stay in the Arctic the whole year round. One January, whilst in the high Arctic, I was astonished to hear a faint chirping, which I could not believe came from a bird until I saw the delicate little creature fluttering in front of me. It was a whiteish-coloured, sparrow-like finch, with a contrasting red hat. The males also have a faint rosy tinge on their breasts. It is the only genuine high Arctic song bird and looks far too frail to winter in those icy, inhospitable surroundings. But it can because it is a plant-eater and, luckily, quite a number of shrubs protrude above the snow or grow in snow-free spots. Thus the red pol does not have the problem of the ptarmigan, or the musk ox, which have to dig their way down through the layers of snow to reach their food. It is extraordinary how this small bird prefers the inaccessible highlands of North Greenland, but it does so because those regions have the willow scrub which is necessary for it. It could easily move south to the warmer climate but it likes to frequent the slopes and mountainsides where, in summer, the temperature is actually higher than at sea level and thus allows the small shrubs to grow taller. The bird of course knows that the winter of the high Arctic is not the white hell so often described by some people, usually those describing the unknown. Most writers on the Arctic are travellers and explorers who, of necessity, are unable to travel during bad weather conditions, and therefore sit in their tents and make the most of their discomfort! I know the winter is not so bad and can remember some glorious days in January when I spent the winter months at 75 degrees north.

"Do you know," I said to Rory, trying to capture his attention for fear that he might frighten the birds away, "the red pol is the only bird in Greenland that builds its nest in a shrub. All the others make their homes on the ground."

The red pols were chirping to each other from the bushes in a peaceful, subdued way, as if they were afraid of breaking the silence of the Arctic scene. As I listened I caught the note of another bird song: the wheatear. I espied its white rump as it flitted among the shrubs, singing as it flew. It rose higher, silently moving from side to side, then climbing vertically before spreading its wings and descending, emitting a trilling song on the move.

The singing and chirping of the birds had poured life on to the hillside which, until then, had seemed quite devoid of animal life. We had seen no hare, no musk ox, no bears, no reindeer, not even an Arctic fox. Had it been so desolate in the Viking days? The bones we had seen in the middens we had scraped at had indicated far more wild life in their day. However, there could not have been so much more for the land would not stand it. I am sure that this meant the Vikings had to travel long distances inland to procure their food. The Eskimos, of course, had always lived like this, and they had no need to return home at the end of each day, for, like a snail, they took their houses with them.

"Come on," said Rory, picking up the thread that was in my mind. "We've got to get back to the tent. I'm getting sodden in this drizzle."

5

A PTARMIGAN CHIRPED me awake; and it was not long before we were away. I was so stiff after the previous day's ascent of the mountain that a few minutes in the canoe soon had me wanting to get out to straighten my legs. But it was good to be off and into the fjord. Our first job was to round the spit but, as the water was shallow (as usual we had set off when we were ready and had not waited for the high tide which would have been best), I was aground. I could feel the canvas graunching on the shingle beneath me. Too late to push off. There was nothing for it but for me to clamber out and to lift the front of the canoe back into deep water. Then I had to leap to get back into it without overturning. I did not mind Rory or myself getting a soaking, but I could not bear to think of the effect of a saturated sleeping bag. It passed without a hitch and soon we had rounded the spit. Huge icebergs, the largest yet, were sailing majestically before us. One was as clear as glass and had blue translucent streaks; others were merely white. It was a flat, calm and beautiful scene.

"Why are those icebergs different?" asked Rory turning round.

"It depends on how much air is trapped inside," I explained. "That hissing noise you can hear as you pass them is the air escaping. When all the air has been expelled then it becomes clear, like that one over there. The really white ones, those that look like chunks of snow, have recently broken away from the glaciers; which is where they all come from anyway, of course. All these 'bergs come from the point where the ice cap stretches into the fjord, just round the corner. You remember, where we saw it from the mountain yesterday. These Greenland glaciers are fast moving and so there are always more and more 'bergs peeling off into the sea. When we get to the entrance to the fjord you will find larger and larger ones."

"It's going over," shrieked Rory, interrupting me.

Sure enough, the huge iceberg heaved slightly, as if shrugging its shoulders, and then slowly and regally sank out of sight, to surface a few seconds later showing a great jagged edge.

"Nothing happens quickly you said, Mum. Remember?" said Robin, laughing at me. "Do you see the canoe-catcher underneath that iceberg?"

He was right. A great finger of ice jutted in our direction. A few feet closer to the iceberg and we would have been caught. We paddled on, out into the fjord. The lower reaches of yesterday's mountain towered above us. As we progressed I became aware of a line in front of us. What was it? A bore wave? It was on us in an instant. Wind! Immediately we were being battered, and the waves were breaking into the cockpit; water sloshed about my knees. I could not stop to bale, for if I did so we would soon be blown over.

"Head for that island ahead," I shouted to Robin. "We should get some lee on the inner side."

White horses reared up between us and the shore. We'll never make it, I thought, fighting with my paddles to propel us forward. The water was now spiralling about us and frantically I paddled towards the small island.

"No good, Mum," cried Robin over his shoulder. "It's attached to the land. We'll have to go round."

Again he was right. We were forced out into the open fjord. We couldn't turn round and head to the shore because of the strength of the wind: sideways on it would have bowled us over. It battered at my lifted paddle. Oh disaster! the red plastic bag which topped the load was saturated. It was the sleeping bag. Another wave broke right over us, dousing the rucksack that I kept between my knees. That's the flower book and the cameras wet, I thought, as I drove my arms to go faster.

Robin and Rona had drawn ahead and were now turning the island; I could see their canoe sideways on to the waves, with white water all around as the sea broke over it. Then they were out of sight. Rory was useless; cowering down in the canoe with his hands over his face and his paddle lying lifeless.

"Hang on to your paddle," I yelled at him. "For heaven's

sake keep hold of it; I shall never catch it if it goes overboard."

At last we too were round the island. The only place to go was straight ahead. The shore line came out to meet us and this was about two miles ahead. The water was now spiralling about us: we were in a whirly. I could see nothing, only feel the water slapping against my face. That too passed and the sea sank down. The sun shone brightly. The sea was still rough but Robin had reached the land. I breathed a sigh of relief as I saw him lifting his canoe on to a little beach. We were at least half an hour behind them but as we approached we could see the two of them unloading. Can there be room for a tent there? I thought. From where we were the beach seemed minute. But soon the billowing canvas took the form of our house and by the time we drew alongside it was up.

"Just enough room for it," shouted Robin. "It's a bit boney as this is an Eskimo tent circle, and I cannot move all the boulders. I'm saturated; let's light the primus and dry off."

His face was white and his lips blue; I could also see that Rona's teeth were chattering. In spite of the sun I was frozen to my marrow; the water after all was not much above freezing point, and we all had had a liberal dousing in it. I thought of the Eskimos who spent hour after hour in their kayaks. A wet-suit was the answer to canoeing in Greenland waters; and the Eskimos, of course, had had these for many hundreds of years. They made them from the intestines of whales which are waterproof. They cut a hole for the face and thread a draw string to pull it tight; they do the same for the arms. The skin is then carefully fitted over the cockpit of the kayak so that the Eskimo sits in a sort of waterproof bag.

Wherever there were Eskimos there were kayaks: Canada, Alaska and all over Greenland; even the reindeer Eskimos of the Canadian interior had them. For thousands of years the kayak formed an integral part of the Eskimo's life: a hunter's tool developed to perfection. The earliest ones found are identical to those still in use today, and there is no difference between the kayak implements used then and now. The fact is that 2,000 years ago the kayak had come to the ultimate point of development. Only the construction differed slightly and this merely to suit the particular environment in which it was used. For instance, the kayaks of south Greenland would be stronger and higher above the sea, being designed for the stormy weather and open seas of this region; whilst the kayak in use farther north was shaped for use in ice among which there is no rough water.

The Greenland kayak is normally about fifteen feet long, slightly shorter than the canoes we were using. It is much slimmer, being tailor-made at the middle to fit the hips of the owner. The pieces of wood that form the hull or the skeleton link up and intertwine in such a way that allows the whole canoe to give without breaking up. The pine for the kayak comes from the driftwood which is swept up on the virtually treeless shores of east and west Greenland from the distant reaches of Russia. Drifting for such a long time in icy water the wood becomes impregnated, which seems to make it stronger than normal. The only long piece of wood required for the kayak is for the keel, which is kept in place by the bulkheads, and these can be made from juniper. There is neither metal screw nor nail in the entire canoe, for everything is tied together with strips of sinew in order that the craft will "snake" through the water.

My bottom was stiff and I thought of the lucky kayaker with his fur-lined seat; and, with his fur-lined seal-skin kamiks, or boots, and his seal-skin trousers, he would be much better off than I. In the olden days he would also have had a vest and pants made from bird skins with feathers on the inside. Even so, all that separated him from the icy water was, in fact, no more than a few layers of seal skin. The Eskimo's main advantage over me in keeping warm was his ability to switch off his mind from the cold. I wondered whether all the comforts, luxuries, art, science, technology and wealth of our sophisticated civilization can compensate us for the loss of this great ability of the Eskimo. Many of our so-called achievements have, in fact, been at the expense of such primal skills; progress has deprived us of them. Our intellectual culture is an urban one and yet many of us seem to hanker after, and need, the great outdoors. It is interesting that poets and other artists have invested such glamour in fields and meadows, animal life, the skies, sun and moon, as if yearning for our original environment. I suspect that this romantic inclination, which is at the heart of all art, may be nothing more than a neurosis due to the constraints placed on our bodies by a city life.

The wind still tore at us whilst Robin and Rona helped Rory and me ashore. The indentation in the cliff where we had landed was caused by the delta of a river; the same river that had gouged its way through the rocks we had scrambled over yesterday. All the gravel and soil that it had collected on its downward journey was spewed out into the sea at this point.

"Come and light the primus now," said Robin, "I'm freezing."

As I followed him up the bank I couldn't help but think how vulnerable the tent looked: one tiny dot of colour on a windswept, God-forsaken, stretch of coastline. The horizon was empty: we were absolutely alone. Once inside the tent, though, the loneliness vanished, for it gave us the feeling that we belonged, that we had somewhere to go. Robin handed me the matchbox with a shaky hand and in a few minutes the children could hear the most important sound of our limited world: the roar of the little stove as it sprung into life. We stripped off our cagoules and our sodden jerseys; even my underpants were saturated.

Warm and cosy now, all seemed right with the world. And, as a feeling of drowsy relaxation swept over me, I couldn't help thinking of Nansen's description of people living just as we were when he landed on the east coast of Greenland in 1884.

Nansen was the Norwegian explorer who first had the idea of ski-ing across Greenland from east to west. It was whilst he was making his way up what he thought to be the uninhabited east coast that he encountered a strange, wild and shaggy-looking group of people, dressed in furs. When they saw him they stared and pointed at him, "uttering a bovine sound" which Nansen said was as if "a whole herd of cows were about him". This was obviously a welcome for they rushed towards Nansen indicating a good landing place for his boat. On all sides he was greeted with beaming faces and he was conducted to their camp site. He was surprised to find that these people could be so comfortable in their homes amid the ice and rocks. There was a communal tent from which an enticing glow emanated, and, by means of signs, he was invited in. Accepting the invitation, he passed through the door flap—a curtain of thin membranous skin—and found himself in a cosy room. But his immediate attention was riveted by a highly acrid smell which was derived from a combination of sources. The "powerful odour" from the burning oil lamps, wrote Nansen, was "well tempered with human exhalations of every conceivable kind, as well as the pungent effluvia of a certain fetid liquid which was stored in vessels here and there about the room and which, as I subsequently learnt, is, from the various uses to which it is applied, one of the most important and valuable commodities of Eskimo domestic economy." In other words: urine. Nansen's Eskimos had their fire in a hollow in the floor which kept the temperature consistently at body level, and they all slept together on a raised platform to keep warm.

My eyes began to smart as Nansen's had, but my irritation was the result of paraffin fumes not urine.

"Where's the pricker?" asked Robin. "You put it in the matchbox, but it isn't there now."

At that point the primus spluttered and went out.

"Oh God," I said, "surely it hasn't let us down already."

Under the usual camping conditions a primus runs for ever, but perhaps we had managed to get water into the paraffin. The children looked at me rather worriedly. I had so often impressed upon them that the primus was the source of life in the Arctic and that without heat one would very soon freeze in this environment.

"We will have to light a driftwood fire," I said backing towards the tent door hastily as my own teeth had begun to chatter.

"Is this what you are looking for?" asked Rory nonchalantly, fishing in his pocket and producing the vital pricker. "I just found it among the Eskimos' stones."

Soon the primus was roaring away again and all was well. The water in our clothes soon turned into a warm fog of steam, occasionally dripping on to the flame which reacted with a yellow spurt. Determined to produce more heat I pumped vigorously on the primus which was soon sending out as much heat as it was able. Satisfied, I sank back on my heels, happy with my lot. Our life was reduced to its most simple terms, as stark as the landscape of the sea and the naked rock. We consider that the refinements that are now so much part of the Western culture are essential to our lives; yet here we were living like Eskimos who I knew for a fact were far superior to me when it came to coping with the environment. Although they have no theatres, cinemas, television, practically no music or literature, in fact no science and inventions, they have all that one needs to live. Glancing at the children, I could see that they were as happy as I. They were not yearning for anything.

Rory sensed me looking at him: "Tell us a story, Mum," he urged.

My mind was a blank. "Well," I said, thinking frantically, "there once was a wave." The noise of the sea pounding our small beach had become more and more evident over the hissing of the primus. "It lived in the middle of the Atlantic and was very bored. It drifted slowly west, wandering about without listening to its mum who told it to be careful. One day, when it had moved farther from home than usual, it saw something moving very fast, so went closer to see more clearly. It didn't realize that this was the dangerous Gulf Stream. Before it knew what was happening it had been whisked up by the slip stream of this mass of water, which tore through the sea at a vast speed, moving far too fast for our wave to get off. Nothing for it but to cling on tight. Because the Gulf Stream was far warmer than the wave's usual North Atlantic sea, it began to sweat. Also it could not understand what the Stream was saying, for it only spoke Spanish, coming as it does from Mexico. As the Stream was turning round and round, following the direction in which the earth turns (the same way as our watches go), the little wave's head began to spin. It found itself birling in an easterly direction. The Gulf Stream itself was hurrying north as fast as it could go. The first intimation the wave had of this was when it stopped sweating and began to grow cold. It rubbed its eyes wondering at the pieces of ice that it could see being whisked in another direction. Suddenly the rushing stopped. 'Where are we?' it said to a passing fish. 'Oh, in the Arctic. Don't you know?' it said from a very wide mouth. 'We're very deep down, but this is the terminus of the Gulf Stream. You had better go up and turn left and then you will reach the land. I can't show you the way because I like being down here in the warmer waters of the Gulf Stream. You have to follow that green, sludgy stuff to get to the land. The birds will show you. None of them seems to like the warm water, preferring the icy cold stuff.' Well, the little wave was lonely but he managed to follow the birds until he found himself in a steep cliffy fjord just round the corner from Cape Farewell in west Greenland. He saw some colour on the shore as he headed for it, but when he reached it he found he could not climb out of the sea. Listen, do you hear him lapping against the shore?"

We could only just hear the waves now, which meant that the wind had lessened. I opened the flap door and poked my head out. Flat calm.

"It's like the smile on the face of the tiger," I said to Robin. "Who would have thought that a few hours ago we were in such desperate straits?"

Rory shoved his head out below mine. "Let's come here when there's a war on," he said, sensing the timeless tranquillity of the scene.

"Let me out," urged Rona, pushing from behind. "I want to jump down from the bank onto the sand."

The previous winter, "Hot Dogging" had come to Scotland. This is a type of gymnastic ski jump, where one leaps off a small rise and turns cartwheels and somersaults in the air before landing on one's feet. Rona now did the same, landing in the soft sand. Robin joined her. Taking advantage of their absence I dug out my book; but I was not able to read more than a paragraph or two at a time before one or other of them would interrupt with a "Watch this, Mum. It's called a 'helicopter'." Every twirl and foot position had a name. The traditional

Scandinavian type of jump has never appealed in Scotland. No one is interested in launching themselves off a 25-foot ramp with a run-in of a quarter of a mile. If there's that much snow about, let's ski on it, is the accepted view. This "Hot Dogging", however, is something else. The name identifies the source: American, of course. The back scratcher, for instance, is a matter of crossing the skis, tips to the head, and unwinding in time to land on both feet and come to a controlled stop. Then there is the "iron cross", "double somersault", "spread eagle" or a "daffy"; and one is not allowed to mow down the on-lookers.

"Look at this, Mum," yelled Robin, "it's called a 'half mule', see."

"You showed me that last time," I shouted back.

"No, that was an 'outrigger'."

"Stop, stop," cried Rona. "I've got a new game."

She had found a narrow plank and propped this up between the top of the bank and the sand, rather like a chute. She then stood on the top end and slithered down whilst standing upright.

"You go faster if your gym shoes are sandy," she said. "It works like ball bearings and feels as if you are roller skating."

The sun was now lost behind a bank of cloud that was creeping down the fjord from the north. Now and then the sun flamed out in a great finger of light that shone on the icebergs in the bay, touching them with unbelievable glory. I stirred myself to collect some driftwood as we only had a limited supply of paraffin and obviously needed to keep that for emergencies. This would not be the last time we would get a soaking. As we were now reaching the end of the fjord we could expect to encounter rougher seas.

The far side of the fjord was now shrouded in mist, its stark black mountains softened by wisps of fog; and now and then, as the mist shifted, the sun threw a golden light on a pinnacle or slab of rock. I wandered over to the river, which was of course quite dry, the snow having long since disappeared. As I gazed across the rough gravel of the river bed, I could see that the sky, sea and the slopes of the tundra were the colours of pale blue and lavender and all suffused with a golden light. The large icebergs had been blown close inshore and through their gaps and "keyhole windows" I could see the far-off cliffs on the other side of the fjord and between them the broad valleys which led inland. It was warm now, as warm as home, but, as I saw the shadow of the nearest mountain beginning to edge nearer, I realized it would soon chill. I hastily began to build the fire and soon was crouching down with a match at the ready. One strike and my pile of driftwood sprang to life—and just as soon died. My lips were too sore to blow and so I returned to the tent and once more lit the primus. I leant against the now dried sleeping bag and read while the children came in one by one and settled contentedly by my side. If we were cats, I thought, we would purr.

The next morning was ominous with storm. The hills were dark against a livid lemon sky, the dark stratified clouds that hung over this were so thick that they were only lit from below. I crawled out of the tent but had scarcely time to stand before a rain squall came in and in a few minutes it was raining steadily and blowing hard. Remembering the *fohn* I went round the tent placing the Eskimo boulders carefully on each of our pegs. That will confuse the archaeologists, I thought. They will wonder why the shape of the Eskimo house has changed. The wind was wailing by this time and the canvas of the tent was billowing; at any moment it seemed it would either take off or be torn to shreds. At ten o'clock the wind subsided and when I looked out of the tent, the scene was fresh and clear, a warm sun was drying the newly-washed earth. With a heavy surf breaking along the shore I realized that we would be stuck here for a while; we were not going to be able to paddle through that lot.

"Look," cried Rona, "water is flowing in the river bed." She ran across and shouted back, "It's just right for washing. There's a basin here for soaping, and another for rinsing." The stream, I found, was falling in stepping-stages.

For the first time since we began our expedition I took off my shirt and gave it a good washing in Rona's stream. The cold wind soon whipped it dry and, by the time the sea was calm enough for us to depart, I was wearing it once again.

Rory crouched on a boulder holding the canoes while Robin carefully loaded them up, standing knee deep in the icy sea. We made our way slowly down the coast between the enormous icebergs which, like us, were moving down the fjord with the tide. I decided to take a photograph:

"I must get a photo of that one with you in it," I shouted to Robin and Rona. But, just as they positioned themselves for me to click the camera, the whole iceberg began to move. As Rona paddled frantically backwards, the 'berg slowly sank and then rose again. The icebergs were all shapes and sizes: one seemed to sport two huge wings, another looked like a vast sailing ship.

After two hours we decided to land to stretch our legs.

"What a lovely place!" exclaimed Rona. "Let us stay here."

A perfect harbour had been formed between two fingers of smooth rock, and, clambering over them, we found that the ground was purple with berries. The best yet!

"What are those?" asked Rory, pointing to some little stone walls.

"They look to me like the things we see on the grouse moors at home," I replied.

And that is exactly what they were, I realized: shooting booths. When we crouched down behind the small wall, we could see that any animal going up the fjord would make a perfect target.

"They would be used for seals," I explained. "During the winter, when the fjord begins to freeze, they come towards the land following the ice. Closely behind them would be the bears, for the seals are their main diet. The Eskimo would be unable to use his kayak in the winter as they are too fragile to break the ice; anyway, the kayak was never designed for chasing. The Eskimo was so familiar with the habits of his prey that he was always in position either to surprise from behind or to ambush it; from his knowledge of their routes and precisely where the current tended to make them surface. From the kayak the

Eskimo managed to catch not only seals but walrus and even whales up to about 30 feet."

But more and more of the Greenlanders are now using motor boats which has upset the seals, forcing them to change their habits. It has made them shy and they have altered their routes, thus making it more difficult for the modern hunter than his predecessor. Despite its many advantages there are still some situations in which the kayak is superior to the motor boat. For instance, the kayak is more manoeuvrable and can therefore zig-zag in and out of the thicker ice, as well as allowing the paddler to escape difficult situations by rolling his craft, bottom up and head down, until either the heavy surf or a wave from a collapsing iceberg has passed, after which he can right his canoe. This is not something that the outboard motorist can do!

Behind us there was flat pasture land, a kind of low-level moor. A few scraggy sheep were wandering about, looking rather like Icelandic jerseys with their shades of black and brown.

"Here's some wood for the fire," said Rory, crouching down and pulling at a straight plank. As it moved there was a loud thud, the big flagstone above it jamming down and narrowly missing Rory's fingers.

"It's a trap," said Robin.

He was right. As we looked closer we could see that there was a long piece of sinew attached to the wood with a small fragment of bone at the other end.

"I know what that's for," I cried. "That sinew would be coiled up with a piece of meat pierced by that sharp bit of bone. The idea being that a fox or wolf would eat it curled as it is, swallowing it easily as it would be frozen into a coil. Once inside the animal's stomach the sinew would thaw out and unwind exposing the sharp bit of bone which would then jam in the body. It would not be long before the poor animal would die."

Looking around we could see that there were many similar traps dotted about.

"Why did they want to kill all those foxes, then?" queried Rory. "After all, they don't eat the Eskimo children or anything like that."

"No," I explained, "but if they do eat the sheep, and if you are going to safeguard your sheep you must kill off the foxes. Personally, I think the foxes are useful as they eat up all the waste from the dead seals, and they also deal with the sewage problem, which again is helpful in a land of permafrost.

"I love the little Arctic fox: it is much smaller than you would expect, not much bigger than a cairn terrier from home. We haven't seen any on this trip, so far, which goes to show that these traps must be fairly effective. I have often camped further north in Greenland and it would be quite impossible for you to leave any food outside the tent, for it would soon be gobbled up by the foxes. On one occasion, I remember, I was sleeping out and, because of the foxes, I had placed all my food in a bag which lay close to my head. Even so I woke in the night with a fox actually standing over my face chewing away at my breakfast. I was very worried at that time, for the foxes were reputed to have rabies and it could easily have sunk its teeth into my face."

It was late in the evening now with a glorious low light which lit the pink hills beyond, whilst off shore the giant icebergs rested silently. Suddenly my eyes detected a movement in the water: it was a rowing boat, slipping slowly through the painted picture in front of me. The figure in the boat was sitting forward in the Eskimo way, which seems so much more sensible than the daft European method of facing back to front. The boat flitted past, causing merely a ripple on the surface. The man was round and squat with black hair, and he was wearing a jersey of blacks, browns and greys, exactly the same colours as the sheep behind us. Already he had noticed us, and, as he waved, his round face broke into a great smile. He did not seem surprised or concerned at our presence; he probably knew all about us already. I wonder where he had come from and where he was going. It had taken us two weeks to make our way from Erik the Red's farm and yet we were no more than half way to the settlement at Narssaq.

There was no breath of wind as we sat round our small fire outside the tent. Robin and Rona were playing chess whilst Rory fiddled with a collection of bullets or cartridge shells that he had gathered from the earth in the shooting booths.

"Give you a game, Mum," he said later as the others' game drew to a close.

"All right," I said, thinking of a pleasantly relaxed and easy game. But my wits were blurred by the beauty around me and Rory beat me in five moves! "The Vikings played chess, you know," I told the children. "Many sets have been found in graves and ruins, and in the museum in Iceland I have seen some pieces taken from a grave near here. They also played a kind of draughts, but that game needed 24 round pieces of bone and dice, which were usually carved from cow horn. Nobody knows quite how to play the game; but the main piece, which represented a man, a sort of half-man half-god figure, was larger than the rest and carved from whale bone. Strangely enough, the word the Vikings used for the board, 'taflbord,' is nearly the same as in Welsh. In a ship that was dug up some time ago, and dating about 900, a board was discovered which was marked out for a different game on either side. Games have been found in Ireland, the west coast of Scotland and the Isle of Man, which goes to prove that even the wild plunderers that raided our shores had time for a game of chess in their tents at night."

During the night I was constantly woken with the roaring noise of the collapsing icebergs. The atmosphere being so much warmer now that we had travelled so far from the ice cap, I, like the icebergs, was feeling the heat; the children, too, were restless and thrashing around in the sleeping bag, making it hotter still.

As soon as we were awake we were out of the tent and, in half an hour, we had filled the large billy can with berries; we filled our bowls with them for breakfast. They were so sweet they needed little sugar and we covered them with the powdered milk which we had whipped into a froth. Delicious!

"I wish we had enough fat to keep them as the Eskimos do," I said. "There is just no way that we can take them home."

It is actually the small black berry that the Eskimos prefer to the more succulent blaeberry. They pour molten fat, seal for preference, over the berries; this cuts out the air and thus they remain preserved for many months.

"We must look like the scraelings," I said laughing, as I looked at our mouths: all were deep purple from munching the berries.

6

MANY IDYLLIC DAYS were passed as we slowly made our way down the ever widening fjord, picking our route through the vast icebergs.

"Look how fast we are going," pointed out Rory, as we paddled along early one morning.

He was right: we were travelling at a great rate. Tide race! All the water in the fjord had to squash through a narrow opening to the sea ahead, and with six-foot tides this meant a great deal of water. I was frightened. Supposing the race ended in a whirlpool? What of the ice? Our two canoes shot along towards the kicked-up water ahead, relentlessly swept over the waves as if descending the rapids in a river. I clutched at the sides of the canoe as there was little point in paddling; my feeble efforts would have had no effect against the current. The far side of the fjord was getting closer with every minute as the two sides converged; and, looking ahead, it was difficult to visualize an opening out to sea, for the two walls of rock appeared to merge into one. We were moving faster than the surrounding icebergs which, being deeper, offered more resistance to the rushing water. I was terrified of colliding but, when this seemed inevitable, instants before the crash we would be swept around the 'berg. Rough rocks were closing on our starboard side and it seemed impossible that we should avoid them. Suddenly we shot through and round the point, finding ourselves looking north at a new fjord system. We were close to the settlement of Narssaq.

The current had cast us aside by now and we could paddle where we wished. Thankfully I turned in the direction of the shore. Small splodges of colour were dotted around the brown landscape which, as I drew closer, I made out to be bent figures slowly moving over the tundra. Greenlanders picking berries. One of them caught sight of us.

"Kayakers," he shouted.

People gathered, running to see. Small brown tinker-like tents were scattered along the shore. Nansen had described it all. Although the Eskimos have been in Greenland for some 2,000 years, the Vikings would never have seen such a scene as this. The Eskimos had moved away from this area when the Norsemen were farming the slopes, sending only marauding or spying parties to the Viking settlements to see what there was. I wanted to push on for Narssaq but could not resist the temptation to land here where I knew we would be so welcome. The people saw us change direction and rushed down to the water to help us ashore. They looked with approval on Robin and prodded the muscles of his arms; they fondled Rory's hair and ran their hands over Rona's cheeks. They see many Europeans, of course, for all the Greenland officials are Danes, as are the doctors, architects, nurses, engineers, harbour masters and sea captains. We, however, had arrived like one of themselves; it was our canoes that made us so welcome. Us they could understand, moving as a family from place to place collecting the berries and living off the fish, but the Danes were still an unfathomable quantity to them. They could not understand this habit of working for money, and owning more things than were necessary, or even building a larger house than was required. Similarly they thought it strange to grow more vegetables in the garden than one required to eat, and they could never fathom the need to move on, embarking on a ship and going away. The Danes are constantly trying to change the Greenlanders, encouraging them to go to school, to clean their teeth, to visit the doctor, to stop drinking and to swallow their vitamins. The Danes are by nature serious, whereas the Greenlanders treat life as a huge joke. With nature against you what can you do but laugh?

When we reached the tents we found a very smokey fire, which is caused by their using green rather than dead wood. An enormous blackened pot sat in the middle of the smoke but with our approach it was drawn aside. Everyone gathered around laughing and joking with each other. When I could I joined in.

Robin unfolded the map and traced our route down the fjord, to the great interest of the men and the boys. He pointed to one camp site and from that one of the men was able to indicate the rest of the places we had stopped.

"What do you think is in the pot?" asked Rory.

"Smells like fish," I replied.

Noticing our interest an old woman, who only had two teeth in her mouth, immediately dipped her hand into the pot and passed Rory a large hunk of fish. It dripped between his fingers as he nibbled at the corner.

"It's all right," he said in surprise, a smile spreading slowly across his face.

The Greenlanders loved this and started to dip into the bowl and hand out bits all round. Large strings of greenery, rather like celery, were floating in the pot as well. They were for eating too, and, as I tasted a piece, I realized they were angelica, the large umbilifera that we had seen growing around all the old Viking sites. It added great flavour to the boiled cod. The eyes, bones, tails and scales had all gone into the pot. The method was to shove them all into your mouth and then spit out the non-edibles. Robin did this with great gusto, and was immediately a favourite.

"Look what they're fishing with," he said to me, pointing to a girl who was standing out on some rocks. She spun a length of string round and round her head and then let go. It sailed through the air and landed in the water about twenty feet off shore. Slowly she pulled it in and, sure enough, a large, wriggling silver form was on the one hook.

"What on earth do we carry that fishing rod around for?" Robin said.

I remembered the sophisticated reels and rods that we had seen being carried by the tourists at Narssarssuaq. They were fishing for fun. These people for their very life. All that gear was obviously quite unnecessary.

"*Kaffimik?*" asked the old woman.

"*Kuanak*," I replied, just longing for a cup.

Our Eskimo was limited to "useful" words but I had quite a vocabulary of these which get me by. Grammar is not all that important in Eskimo anyway, as the language is formed by putting together many words. Such compound words are easily separated into their elements which can be juggled about and used for a new construction. In this way, knowledge of a few words can give one far more mileage than in a language such as French! One hundred thousand people speak Eskimo. Often, when Europeans hear someone speak this language for the first time, they are surprised that there is nothing at all that they recognize. Also they are often completely baffled by the length of some of the words. For instance, "*takusinnaassannguat-siartara*", which means "I think I will be able to see it".

The people in the south, here in the Cape Farewell area of Greenland, speak a slightly different dialect from that which I was more accustomed to in the north-west. The phonetic differences between the dialects are quite regular, which means that once one realizes what they are, it is quite easy to understand.

Language in Greenland has been written down ever since the early eighteenth century, with the arrival of Hans Egede, and this long tradition has built up a mass of literature that is unmatched among the indigenous peoples of the New World. There has been a newspaper in Greenlandic since 1861; a strong contrast to the situation in North Canada where the Eskimos were still struggling with the missionary hieroglyphics of triangles, circles and squares right up to 1965. And as I watched Robin and Rona now trying to talk to the people I thought of the tragedy of the Canadian Eskimo's language: although they had attended school in the Canadian North-West Territories their ability to speak was no greater than mine. The Canadian government considers it far better for the Eskimo children to speak English as soon as possible, so only this language is taught in the schools. Whereas here in Greenland, the Danes have been most careful to encourage the children to retain their own language and literature and only teach Danish as a subject, not as a vehicle for basic information.

The women now began hammering with a stone on a piece of cloth that had been carefully laid out on another one.

"What are they doing now?" asked Rory.

"Grinding the coffee beans," I said.

The small quantity of beans was mixed with some barley then tipped into a blackened kettle and stirred over the flames until at last it smoked and the beans roasted. A woman sat on the ground with the kettle between her legs and pounded the beans into grain. Boiling water was then poured over and brewed up with chicory. Little white china cups were produced and the thick, inky brew poured in. A packet of sugar was handed round and I placed a lump between my teeth, sipping the coffee through. In this way the flavour is retained and the sweetness picked up. The cups were refilled and passed round from one to the other. I sat back, absolutely happy. The calm water of the fjord and the stretches beyond, which bent round opening towards the sea, reflected the numerous icebergs that lay in it. Across from this camp site were low mountains with a valley leading inland. Behind us I was conscious of distance. The country felt vast. There was a touch of autumn around. The leaves of the creeping berry plants were bright yellow and scarlet. The people had been picking the berries. They lay spread out on cloths outside the tents. The women were lithe and graceful as they bent over the little piles to clean them of leaves and pieces of twig. The men were still eating out of the communal pot, taking huge mouthfuls between their teeth. If a piece was too big they cut it off with a pocket knife, drawing the blade upwards as near as possible to the end of their nose; then they would spit out the bones into the middle of the circle of people.

I was reluctant to go, but felt that we must push on as it would be difficult finding a camp site within the settlement at Narssaq. Today was the first date on which Hugh might arrive, so we must be there, camping.

"Stay with us, stay with us," said the women as we stood up to go. I could feel their happiness and genuine pleasure at encountering us, yet I knew that we were the lucky ones. What a privilege to have had this short time among these people.

There was hardly room for us in the bay. Vast icebergs had floated in with the tide. There was a stiff wind but the water had only a ripple on the surface—one compensation for the 'bergs. Rowers flitted past us as we zig-zagged our way towards the point behind which we knew nestled the village of Narssaq. Clump! One of the huge 'bergs had collapsed just behind us. We paddled quickly but the one in front was doing the same! We changed direction, heading further out than I intended; but there was nothing for it, we had to round the point. The calm water gave us a sense of security. Round the corner—and there was Narssaq.

Dull red or green or blue houses nestled around the bay. Their muted colours were part of the scene. I thought of new towns, like Cumbernauld, which are such a jar on the landscape. We headed towards the large pier in the centre of a group of buildings. A recently surfaced blue iceberg was close by.

"Stop," I said to Rory. "I must take a picture. Just look at the colour of that ice."

A loud shout from the shore distracted me and I looked over my shoulder to see a round old Eskimo waving his arms.

"It will fall," he warned.

I couldn't possibly disregard him so we paddled on towards the shore. The old man could see where we were aiming for and was hurrying along a path. Again we heard the shout "Kayakers" and the old man was joined by many children and young men and women. They were all smiling and waving and walked into the water to help us out. People shook hands and bowed and talked to us. We answered in our pidgin Eskimo.

"I love them all," said Rory sensing the warmness surrounding him.

We crouched on the shingle and laid out the map.

"Look out," said Robin. "There are dead fish all over the ground."

Sure enough the shore was littered with the heads and guts of cod. In fact, garbage was all around us, and there was a distinct pong. Nothing to do but ignore it, though!

The people crowded round as we pointed on the map to where we had come from and to where we were going. A horse ambled down and rested its big yellow teeth on someone's shoulder. It was pale brown with a darker mane; similar to the Icelandic ponies one sees in north Scandinavia. It bent its neck and munched at the odd fish head, completely at home in this rather bizarre surrounding.

"Where is the store?" I asked. "The KGH."

These letters stand for The Royal Greenland Trade Company which, until recently, had the complete monopoly on trade in Greenland. It owned the shops and the boats that brought in the supplies. It took this responsibility very seriously. Now not only does it have to supply its own shops but also has to provide for its competitors. Recently the Danish government decided that it would be a good thing if private businesses were allowed to trade; so, as well as the large, organized KGH stores, there are many little shops, small scale and housed in a shack, here and there. Originally the KGH worked rather on the lines of the Hudson Bay Company: trading and bartering for local products, like skins, fish and whale oil, with the Greenlanders. "If you show a Greenlander a gold piece and a sewing needle, he will reach out for the latter," said the mayor of Hamburg in 1740.

German and Dutch captains had found out long ago that trading with the locals, or "savages" as they called them, went more smoothly when they had been given a strong dose of gin. In return for shirts of the cheapest kind, stockings, mittens, tin kettles, knives, awls, fish hooks, glass beads and other cheap trinkets, the European captains obtained seal and whale blubber, whale bones, narwhal tusks and skins of reindeer, fox and seal. When the bartering was finished there would be dancing on deck, while down below the crew made merry with the Greenlanders' wives. The outcome of those days can still be seen in the pale faces of the Greenlanders of the south-west coast. A recent genetic study has shown that half of the population of one township, Holsteinsborg, is of Dutch origin.

Fights, killings and kidnappings went on, as well as barter, between the European captains and the locals as part of the clash of the two cultures. Accusations of robbery, theft and murder were mutual. In 1720 Dutch shipowners were forced to issue a proclamation that "any seafarer who molests, attacks or steals the property of the natives will at first lose his wages and afterwards in proportion to his misdeeds he will be punished as a pirate and public assaulter". This did not do the Greenlanders much good, however, because they were a long way from the law courts in the Hague and there was little in the proclamation to help them. If a Dutch ship was shipwrecked or stranded, however, the Greenlanders might move in and murder the shipwrecked sailors. The Dutch sent about 70 ships into the Davis Strait and bartering took place in particular at the island of Nipisat, about 50 miles up the coast from where we now were. The best whaling grounds in the whole of Greenland were in that area.

In 1726 the Danish government suggested to the Copenhagen merchants that they take over the trade and push out the Dutch. Jacob Sewerin was the first merchant to take up this suggestion, and in 1734 he was awarded a trading monopoly in return for an annual grant of 2,000 Danish rix dollars that he must pay to the Christian missionary, Hans Egede.

Jacob was the son of the town judge from Jutland and at the age of 22 he had married a wealthy 62-year-old widow from Copenhagen, whose dowry made him immediately acceptable among the merchants of the capital. He bought out all rivals in the Iceland trade until he was looked upon as the king of the northern seas, presiding over the trade from his estate in Jutland. On several occasions he complained of the Dutch eating into his profits in Greenland and he persuaded the government to issue a royal embargo forbidding the Dutch to land at any port in Greenland and banning trading inside a five mile off shore limit. Needless to say, many of the Dutch captains ignored this and continued to trade. One shipmaster, Johan Jobs, ignored the Danes but he was seized by Jacob Sewerin's ship and his cargo of wooden boards was used to repair the houses in the new Danish colony. The year after, the Dutch turned up with five armoured ships and declared that it would cost "plenty of blood" if the Danes tried to accost them again. They put into the settlement of Jacobshavn and refused to leave the harbour. Three of Sewerin's ships, including an armoured galleon, anchored outside and at midnight opened fire on the Dutch who, after a good hour's cannonade, surrendered. They were brought ashore and started tackling the gin instead of their captors and by early morning the surrounding hills echoed with yelling and singing as all the Europeans, Dutch and Danes turned the night into an orgy. They had surrendered.

On 8 March 1776 the Danish state took over the monopoly and officially Greenland was closed to private trade. The Royal Greenland Trading Company had a very noble aim, namely; "To the greatest extent possible to safeguard the interests of the natives"; but it would do no harm if it showed a profit as well! This it did, varying from year to year. As an example, from 1829 to 1850 the profit amounted to 1,000,000 Danish krones per year. The economic basis was the whale catch which in certain periods resulted in 2,200 barrels of train oil being shipped back to Denmark plus 18,000 pieces of whale bone. One single whale would give from 200 to 250 barrels of train oil which would be worth about £70 sterling a ton. Anyone living in Copenhagen in those days was well aware of the trade with Greenland, because the burning of whale blubber sent a stench over the entire city!

The two principal managers of the trade in Greenland lived at either end of the area settled by the Danes, and it was their duty to make tours of inspection in their enormous districts. As a rule this took place from an umiak, the name given to the large Eskimo family boat. The manager was a distinguished gentleman who was received in style. An account of 1829 describes how 64 pounds of gunpowder were used that year to salute the inspector. On the other hand, he used 240 quarts of spirits, 170 quarts of malt and 4 lbs of hops for making beer for the Greenlanders on the king's birthday, at Christmas and for a jamboree when there was an exceptionally large whale catch. The names of these inspectors still recur in present Greenland communities, particularly in some of the more well-to-do families living in the settlements on the west coast.

The store at Narssaq was at the other side of the settlement and the people indicated to us that we should put to sea again and paddle right away from the village and round the corner where we would find a long inlet that would lead us right into the heart of the settlement and close beside the KGH store. I wanted to walk but there was no arguing! The people pushed us off again and we paddled right across the bay, keeping a wary eye on a large trading ship anchored at the jetty. I was terrified that its wash when it started to move would make the huge icebergs surrounding us topple.

The children's one topic of conversation was "What would we buy at the store?" Rona hankered for a bottle of Coke. Rory felt like sweeties, and Robin repeatedly pointed out that his feet stuck right out of the bottom of his gym shoes which now had no sole whatsoever. I wanted some bread, remembering a Danish bakery I had visited at another town in the north-west where the smell of Danish pastry and fresh yeast had wafted out into the cold frosty air. I remembered the sticky centre of almond paste as one bit into the flaky pastry. We passed another big ship unloading at an oil depot. The sun was sinking. Supposing the shop is shut by the time we get there? I thought. For the whole journey we had counted time by the rise and fall of the tide. Now we must be more particular. The view was breathtaking. The low light illuminating the entire bay crammed with icebergs. Beyond, a great sweep of inland ice joined the silvery sea. The view was occupied with little boats dotted here and there, motionless and silent, their owners fishing. Now we came to the inlet which made us turn with our backs to the view, as we paddled up the narrow stretch of water with more and more houses forming on either side. No big tankers here. The inlet, though, was crowded with small craft. No kayaks but home-made little boats of all shapes and sizes depending on the amount of driftwood available at the time the owner felt like making a boat.

The tide was out and we had to squelch our way through grey oozy mud to reach the shoreline.

"Leave the boats here, Mum," said Robin, "the tide won't be back for at least an hour or two."

"No, no," I said, "higher, higher."

I was already imagining the marvellous time we were going to spend footling away our money in the store. At last we were able to head for it: a low grey building, unmistakable. Outside a large flagpole had an enormous Danish flag and a sign with a rampant polar bear against a blue shield. Noisy Danish children were crowding us, pushing and shoving. Their parents eyed us askance. The Danes are very conformist and in true colonial tradition did not approve of eccentrics such as us. They were here because they had to be, and they could not understand the attraction of Greenland to people like myself.

We entered the building. Rona and Rory were thrilled. They scuttled off between the counters, fingering this and touching that. Now inside, I could not think of anything. I looked at the little tins of delicacies for making Danish "smorbröd". Why should we want jam when the countryside was full of berries? Or sardines when we had fresh cod? I remembered that we could do with a new map and found the relevant counter. The Eskimo girl wanted to please. She produced more and more of the wrong area. "No, no," I said quoting the number that I needed. "Yes," she said unravelling yet another cylinder of beautiful virgin white cardboard. But her maps were of Denmark, Norway and even one of the world.

"You must buy something," said Rona. "What about Scotland?"

The girl smiled with relief and produced a perfect map. Rory jumped up and down with excitement.

"There's Glasgow," he said. "Look that's where we live."

What could I do but buy it! Then I remembered the primus. I walked over to the shelves of spanners and screws, nuts and bolts, fish hooks and wheels. No good. Another sweet girl with dead pan, oriental face and black, black hair knew exactly what I wanted and led me over to the jewelry counter. She pulled out a tray with gold watch straps and, lying beside them, were rows of primus washers.

"Shoes over there," said Robin pointing to the far corner. He pushed his current gym shoes up to his knee exposing a filthy foot with long grimy toe nails. The Greenland girl serving saw nothing wrong with him trying on various shoes for size, but a passing Dane was horrified.

Rona and Rory were mesmerized by the trappings of civilization in the shop. Robin, on the other hand kept pulling at his polo-neck, overcome with claustrophobia with the heat and mass of people beneath one roof.

"Let's go, Mum," he kept muttering. "The tide could be in."

We drove the others out, then noticed the bakery, separate on the right. The scent of warm bread wafted towards us and we made a rush for the door. The Danish pastries were as I remembered. How could we possibly choose between this or that? At last, outside with bulging bags we could go no further than the step. We sat there munching hunks of bread and nobody asked for butter or jam. There was a bustle of people around an outside store.

"What's going on there?" I asked Robin. "Go and find out. I can't possibly move yet."

He wandered off and soon waved to us enthusiastically.

"Oh," said Rory as we came near, "this is where you get real food."

Rory was right. Huge chunks of meat and fish were lying out while the Greenlanders prodded and poked, and selected slices and cuts. One fish was enormous. A wolf fish, cream with dark leopard-like spots. The yellow flesh was shark and the great chunks of bloody meat must be reindeer, hunted farther north. There was far more animation, life and activity around this stall than anything I had seen inside the sophisticated store.

"Oh, look at that face," said Rory pointing to a little skull with velvet skin. "What is it, Mum?"

I noticed the hairs above the little black nose, and realized it was a seal.

"It's such a nice little face," he said, "I want to feel it."

"It's for eating, you dope," said Robin, "If you're going to buy meat to eat, Mum, buy some of those steaks."

He was pointing to some thick slabs of juicy-looking flesh. The surrounding Greenlanders saw our interest and all came forward with advice. One woman, feeling that I had not paid enough attention, whipped out a knife and cut off a sliver and handed it to me on the point.

"Eat it, Mum, eat it," said Robin nudging me.

I slipped it in my mouth and swallowed hard. "Yes, yes," I said nodding my head, "that will do nicely."

"Taste this, taste this," said another woman cutting off a piece from a different slab.

Terrified that this could continue I hastily produced my envelope of damp Danish krone notes.

"Deal with it," I said to Robin relying on his quicker brain than mine in mastering the foreign currency.

Clutching our dripping meat I wandered off up the street. The houses here were smart, trim, State-subsidized ones. It was a sort of housing scheme. Outside one trim little house squatted an old couple. She was working on a skin, using her curved ulu. She was an ancient old crone and faced us with two teeth hanging over her sunken jaw. Her wizened face cracked into a magnificent smile as she caught sight of us with her poor, failing eyes. She beckoned us with a twisted hand so we stepped forward and knelt beside her skin. Her old man was pegging it out with pieces of rib. He took great care to stretch it exactly. A bucket was close by, oozing intestines with a horror of blue bottles buzzing around. A motorbike passed and a car with a smart Danish driver. I could see telephone wires and even a public box, all of which looked so temporary whereas this old couple seemed timeless.

The Danish government means well and their investment must be without parallel in other developing areas of the world. For a long time though there have been many people questioning the Danish policy in Greenland. Could the social development, for instance, be based to a greater extent on Greenland's own cultural background? The improvements in the Greenland community during the course of the last 100 years or so are indisputable. Hospitals, clean houses, education, variation in food—and social security. The Greenlanders have for centuries been able to adjust themselves successfully to their hostile Arctic homeland and their greatest difficulty today, to a large extent, is a head-on confrontation with the European social pattern. The Europeans' way of life is diametrically opposed to that of the Greenlanders. The competitive society is completely alien to their communal way of life in which everybody works at the common tasks and does what is necessary for the survival of the wide family unit. They are not interested in one-up-manship, or owning more than one's neighbour. The quality of one's seal-skin clothes depended on one's own ability to sew them, not on money for buying better than anyone else. The Danish government's policy and administration is quite understandable, but is it really all necessary? Is it possible to alter the drift towards Western "civilization"? The present material standard of living in Greenland is artificial, created on the strength of the enormous investment of the Danish Treasury. But, luckily for the Greenlanders, the waters and thin soil do not provide nearly enough raw materials to justify anything approaching the standard of living in Denmark. The difficulties facing the government in Copenhagen are exactly the same as that of the Vikings. They vanished off the face of Greenland. Are these modern Danes to go the same way?

"Where will we camp?" asked Robin.

"What about over there?" I said pointing to the edge of the settlement where the brown hills folded down to meet the sea.

"There is a mine down there," said Robin "That's why there are so many of these big boats about. I saw it marked on a map."

"What is being mined?" I asked. "Something to do with aluminium," he answered.

"All right then," I said, "it looks closer to go there than to paddle all the way back to the other side of the settlement, although we want to be there when Dad arrives so that he'll see us."

We wandered back to the canoes and were just about to roll up our trousers to wade over the mud when our friend of that morning arrived. The old man was waving his hands at us, pointing behind him to where we had encountered each other.

"No," we said, "we're going on in the other direction."

He shook his head frantically, and made digging actions.

"He's telling us about the mine," said Rona, quick on the uptake.

"Well, what's wrong with that?" asked Robin.

"Yes, we know there's a mine," I said, "but that won't stop us camping in there will it?"

The old man grew more agitated.

"He doesn't seem to want us to go there," I said. "There must be something funny about it. It's not worth arguing about, anyway. Let's go back to that shelf where we first met the Greenlanders and then we won't have to move until Dad arrives."

The old man was greatly relieved to see us agreeing with his suggestion. He had long sealskin boots which seemed impervious to the mud. I pointed out to him that he was slowly sinking, but he didn't seem to mind in the least. With a great squelchy noise he walked to the bank and we pushed off back into the glorious scene of light on water and ice.

The 'bergs were now pink as we slowly paddled across the absolutely calm water making no sound or ripple on the surface. Nobody spoke. The children sensed the silence that is the great quality of the Arctic. Back past the big harbour and across the bay, the way we had come that morning. We found a ledge just out of sight of the village, with a good landing on shelving slabs. We clambered up the slope of blaeberry shrubs and pitched the tent. There was barely enough room. I had the feeling of toppling out into the sea as I snuggled down into the sleeping bag.

"I brought you a present, Mum," said Robin digging in the bag of goodies from the store. He produced a bottle of Carlsberg and began to attack the lid with his teeth.

"Oh, I can do that," announced Rory, "I learnt this afternoon."

He grabbed the bottle from Robin and his tiny little milk teeth crunched home on the metal. The lid was off and I lay back sipping the froth.

7

I PEEPED OUT of the tent in the morning to a view of vast icebergs in calm water. Was it really the sea? I had a holiday feeling, as we didn't need to get up and move on. Rona and Rory soon scrambled out of bed and went off to catch fish for breakfast. They stood below us, perched on the edge of the slabs, throwing the line. In a minute they were pulling it in in a hurry.

"It's big enough for all of us," they yelled up.

My heart sank. I hated gutting the big cod. Our knife was blunt and it would be quite a struggle to amputate the head.

"You'll have to come," Rona shouted. "I can't get it off the hook."

The large fish was jumping around on the rock threatening to leap off, line and all. Hastily I scrambled down in bare feet. I put my hand gingerly on its body. It leapt into the air with a bigger fright than me. I picked up a stone and threw it. I missed. Then I lost my temper with it for upsetting me and grabbed the fish by its tail. I meant to swing it over my head and bring it down with a thud, but it wriggled and I let go. Robin was thundering down behind me now, already clutching a large rock. He hurled this at the fish and it lay still. I prodded it and, sure enough, it seemed to be dead.

I began hacking with the knife but as I reached the spine the fish shot into the air again. Now I had to finish the job! I put my knee on it and hacked off the head. I raised the knife to cut it into steaks and it jumped again when I severed the spine. Hating it by this time, I tore out its guts then knelt down to wash it in the sea. Gutless and headless it writhed when it touched the cold water.

A flock of snow buntings flitted about round the tent. Was winter arriving already? I thought as I watched them. Sure enough there was a feeling that the tranquil scene was waiting for something.

"Fresh bread," shouted Rona and, remembering this, we all scrambled back up for the tent. Some Greenland children drifted over the tundra from the village, grazing, like sheep. They moved slowly, silently, tundra coloured, eating the berries. As they came closer one picked a plant from a rocky crevice. It was rose root.

"Look what he's eating," said Rory, "Will he die, is it poisonous?"

"Can't be," I said, "he must know what he's doing." Rory ran down towards the children and was soon part of the group.

The ice in the bay was constantly turning. All the 'bergs rolled over. It did not depend on size or shape.

"Do you see, they all have a canoe catcher under the water too?" pointed out Robin.

The biggest and most stable was just as likely to roll over or collapse as the smaller bits of brash. There was a constant noise of frying bacon: the air sizzling out as the ice melted in the warmth of the sun.

In the distance there was the noise of heavy traffic. I sent Robin to see what it was.

"It's three vehicles, sort of dumper trucks, driving to and fro at breakneck speed. There's only one little stretch of road," he pointed out, "between the harbour and the fish factory. I can't think what they are doing."

"I wish, I just wish I were at home," wailed Rory coming back to join us. "Oh to be at home."

"Whatever's the matter?" I asked.

"I'm longing for some fresh milk," he said. "That large store over there and no fresh milk."

After weeks of nothing to buy he now longed for the impossible.

There was a silver grey light on the sea now; no movement, until an iceberg rolled over. A rower slipped through the picture barely ruffling the surface. So beautiful. So silent. I sank back into the tent completely happy. Suddenly a great honking noise rent the air, tearing the peace. A hooter! I had just recovered when it started again.

"It's the fish factory," explained Robin, who seemed to know everything about the settlement already. "I bet it goes again in a minute."

And it did. In fact it went every minute for a quarter of an hour. Obviously the Danes had great trouble encouraging the Greenlanders to come to work. I felt sorry for them, trying to keep the timeless Eskimos up to schedule.

A small boat approached our landing stage. It was full of giggling girls. They clambered out of the boat, came up the slope and crouched around us in a semi-circle, bashful and giggling behind their hands. It took me a few minutes to realize they were not interested in me. All their attention was riveted on Robin. They were trying to make him notice them. Looking rather flustered he was behind me in the back of the tent and I realized he had been quicker on the uptake than I. One of them pulled Rory onto her knee, thinking she might curry favour that way.

I remembered the occasion a few years ago when we had taken twelve Glasgow medical students with us to Iglorsuit, a hunting village far to the north-west. The people lived entirely off the land and I was worried that our presence would upset their way of life. It was not often that twelve handsome energetic young men visited such a place *en masse*. Whatever would happen to the girls? I needn't have worried. It was more a question of whether the students would survive the onslaughts of the locals! They were the ones to protect, and not the other way round.

I did not know how to interfere, so left it to Robin to cope. In a few minutes he sauntered down to the sea. The girls followed him in a crowd. Their silvery laughter and twittering voices rather like the snow buntings. Nonchalantly Robin began to fish, throwing his line in like the locals. The biggest girl took it from him and threw it much further. I began to feel a wallflower so dug out my book. The next time I looked up Robin and his girls were all in the boat. They were rowing, sitting at his feet, flanking him on either side. They were out to please and Robin was loving it. I wondered if British education had taught him how to manage the attentions of so many girls at once. I was quite sure that Hugh had never given him any advice on the mass approach.

"There are just no boys around you know," explained Rona. "I think they must all work at the fish factory."

One of the girls had jumped ashore and ran up the bank for Rory. He loved this attention and pretended to run away, allowing himself of course to be easily caught and carried down to the boat.

"Let's go for a walk," I said to Rona, feeling a bond.

We wandered up behind the tent completely out of sight of the village. There was a movement ahead of us and then a loud quack. It was a goose. Instead of flying away it walked and sat down behind a boulder, then it ran again, flapping some rather scraggy wings. It was moulting, and I remembered that this was the time of the year when they shed their wing quills; a dangerous time for them. I began to chase the goose ahead of me. It ran fast but seemed to tire quickly and kept hiding behind stones.

"Catch it, catch it," urged Rona, but I didn't really want to.

August is the month of moult in the Arctic. This is the last stage through which the birds must go before they depart from their summer home. The life of the birds at breeding places is divided into several periods. First comes mating, courtship and nest-building; then laying, brooding, rearing the young; and finally the period of the annual moult. This is most important in the Arctic because it is usually accelerated in order to be over before the first frosts of the autumn. But a mother bird cannot start until the young ones have reached a certain stage of development. So the drakes start to lose their feathers much earlier than the female geese or duck. It is the same with the cocks of the ptarmigan and grouse. By now, in late summer, no bird had any young except in rare cases when the first brood had been robbed by foxes, or wiped out by flooding or some other disaster. As the young are well on their way to the grown-up stage, the parents can concentrate on the necessary loss of their feathers. The moult is a long process and seems to require all the energy of the bird. It needs new ones to develop as a protection against the cold which is now increasing. They are paler, dense and tight and with them the birds begin to accumulate a thick layer of fat beneath their skin and around the intestines, which is a source of energy during the migration. Many of the Arctic birds do not feed during their flight across the oceans which often begins before the end of August. The little goose in front of us now was as fat as butter.

We soon reached the summit of the little hill. We could now see right round the point, back into Erik's fjord and forward out to the ocean. The settlement was out of sight below us.

"Which way will Dad come?" asked Rona.

"That way of course," I said pointing to the fjord, "but don't let's get excited yet. He can't possibly have arrived in Greenland until late yesterday evening. Remember his conference in Washington didn't finish till the day before yesterday; then he had to fly to New York, then to Rekjavik in Iceland, retracing his steps to Greenland, and then find a boat to bring him down the fjord to Narssaq. All that could take him days and days. I just said he *might* be here today, but I didn't really mean it. I don't think, in fact, he'll be here for at least two more."

"I think you're wrong," answered Rona. "I have a feeling he'll come today."

She was so confident I did not bother to argue.

We wandered farther over towards the settlement, and were soon among the neat wooden houses. The road led, like all of them, to the centre square in front of the KGH store. A very neat Danish official was hammering up a poster. Another was already on the wall. No one was paying any attention, although groups of women were gossiping about the open meat stall and men sitting about, puffing on their pipes.

We peered at the notices, picking out words here and there. One was in Eskimo, and the other Danish.

"*Kafamik*. It's a party," I said. "*Dronigen*—that means queen."

"I know what it is," shouted Rona. "The queen is coming—and here is the date, 12 August at 10 a.m. When's that?"

I had no idea. "Well," I pondered, "Dad's conference ended on the 10th—it must be tomorrow."

That explained the unusual activity we had seen at the factory, of fish heads being carefully swept up, and trucks bustling about, upsetting the tranquil scene.

"Look," said Rona, "there is a man painting his home, and look at the KGH. They're cleaning the windows."

The official was now talking to the men running the meat stall, obviously telling them to clear up the mess. A cloud of bluebottles hovered over it, and blood stained the earth all around. The men looked put out, as if they could not understand what the official was complaining about.

"We must tell the others," said Rona heading back for the tent.

"Yes," I said, "let's go back and see what Robin's doing. I just don't trust him with all those girls."

"Oh, Chopo," said Rona scornfully using her nickname for him. "He's useless. Any other boy would have made himself look nice and combed his hair. He just looks dreadful, like a pirate."

A Greenlander, in a grey and brown jersey, was sitting outside the tent. He looked slightly tipsy. As we came up he smiled in a friendly way and handed me a beer. He had come to see the canoes, we gathered. I downed my beer and then in the same state of mind as him we tripped through the blaeberry bushes down to the upturned boats. He was particularly interested in the plastic-coated canvas skin. He prodded and poked and stretched it and felt it between his fingers and came to the conclusion that it was not nearly as good as the outer cover of his kayak.

"Of course not," I had to say, "but we don't have hours of time to scrape a seal skin, even if we had the opportunity to shoot one in the first place."

Sewing the skin is even more difficult, double stitches have to be made with thread of whale sinew which has first been cut into fine strips and then twined. The old Greenland legends make a point of reminding the hunter never to leave the sewing of the cover for the kayak to an inexperienced woman but always to one whose skill he can trust. The seams have to be constantly greased with whale oil or blubber to keep them flexible and watertight. Then there are the leather strips which have to be attached on the outside, each in a special place, to fasten the various implements to the kayak itself. The Greenlander now fingered our paddle. He thought it far too big to be useful and held it out at arm's length with a laugh. The Greenland kayakers use a very slim paddle so that it makes minimal noise in the water. But at the same time it must be extraordinarily strong. This means that the grain must be at a diagonal angle at the narrowest part of the paddle. The edges of the blade are then reinforced with pieces of bone.

"How could I do all that, living in the centre of Glasgow?" I asked him.

"Where is your harpoon?" he asked turning to Robin who now came up. After all, in Greenland it's only the men that go out in the kayaks. It was the fat bath-shaped umiak that was reserved for the women.

When our visitor realized that Robin did not have a harpoon he took him by the arm and suggested he went back to the village and he would give him one. I felt slightly worried. Obviously much beer would be drunk and what about all those girls, who were still clustering round? The man, not much taller than Robin, took his arm and off they went round the shore towards the village.

"Do you think those are all his daughters?" asked Rona.

"I hope not," I said, remembering that it is an old Greenland custom that the man offers his daughter, not his wife, to the visitor. The old ways were very strict in this respect.

The morning had been grey and sunless but now the clouds lifted and colour and life returned to the scene. The sea sparkled and many boats were pushing out towards the ice to fish. I understood why they rowed facing forward. 'Bergs and brash ice were everywhere and the boats had to pick a course between the pieces of ice. The big ones were always moving, rolling over or slowly subsiding without a sound. Suddenly, a vast bird swooped down and took a fish from our landing place. It was brown with black pinion feathers and a white tail. It slowly flapped its wings and flew to perch on a nearby iceberg looking noble, like the eagle on the American crest.

We peered hopefully at every boat that rounded the point in our direction although I knew that Hugh couldn't possibly be here yet; or could he?

"Go and do something," I said to Rona and Rory, fed up with them playing the waiting game.

Rona couldn't resist the honey pot of shops in the settlement so hand in hand she and Rory wandered back towards the houses. They were close to the fish factory when the hooter went once more and I could see an explosion of people. They were covered in long white coats. As they ran out of the long building they discarded these in an untidy heap on the ground. They jumped the fence and ran down towards the harbour. Each one fiddled in his pocket and dug out a fishing line. They threw these, like a lariat, into the sea and soon pulled out large wriggling fish. Although they had spent so many hours handling the frozen slabs at the factory they could not resist this contact with the real thing. A group of boys threw off their clothes and jumped in beside the fish splashing and shouting exuberantly.

I heard a motor and looked out towards the sea; saw threading its way through the ice, having rounded our point, a large launch. Standing in the front was a man. He was unmistakable—it was Hugh.

I waved and shouted and the boat changed course and headed for the tent. Hugh was wearing his Washington, "going to conference" suit and was carrying a brief-case. His hair, on the other hand, was wild and shaggy. He looked in fact like an explorer dressed up. The crew fended the boat off from the rock as Hugh stepped down, nonchalantly handing me his brief-case. When he reached the tent he opened this and revealed, not conference papers, but his pair of climbing boots.

Rona and Rory sauntered back quite unaware that he had arrived. It was an hour later still when Robin returned with his friend. He was wearing quite different clothes: a new jersey the colours of the sheep and very smart trousers.

"Where did you get those?" I shouted before he had arrived.

"The Greenlanders gave them to me," he answered. "They seemed to think I looked too scruffy and this bag is full of beer.

I have been out in the kayak, eaten seal meat and all those boats you can see out there fishing are home-made you know. They're after those huge wolf fish and each boat has a long knife, like an Amazon machete. The fish are enormous. It would have been frightful if we had caught one from the canoes by mistake."

The Greenlander was also carrying a plastic bag and handed it to me as he sat down outside the tent. It was full of coffee, biscuits, eggs and more beer. Hugh, mesmerized with tiredness, had to sit the evening through. We were going to have to drink all the beer, I could see! More Greenlanders arrived and the conversation, as we sat in the low evening light, was of kayaks and hunting.

"We're camping on Eskimo graves," said Robin to the other children. "Not really on them, because the bodies were just laid out here on top of the ground. When a hunter dies he is brought out here, where he can look out to sea to the best hunting places. It's difficult to dig because of the permafrost so they just pile stones on top of the dead men."

Slowly the darkness gathered, and our horizon shrank to the faces glowing round Robin's little fire. The Greenlanders went back to their huts and we squashed into our sleeping bag. I had forgotten how much room Hugh took up. We had been alone for so long it seemed more natural to be without him. He tossed and turned, complaining of the slope of our camp site. The last time he had been in bed was in a smart hotel in Washington, and was now suffering all the ills of the jet age. We had arrived here slowly, assimilated by the scene, whereas he had been catapulted from civilization.

There was a low mist in the morning. I made pancakes for breakfast with a real egg. What a difference. The sweeping up of the harbour was still going on. Tractors were bustling about and the Danes were hanging up flags. We could see potted plants being rushed down to the pier from the Narssaq Hotel. Fish heads were being swept away and the home-made boats towed off-shore. Only the ice was still untidy. Robin urged us to set off for his friends and eventually we walked along the path below the factory. What a change. It was spruce and clean. No dead fish anywhere. The Greenlanders were looking on with somewhat blank expressions but the Danes were scuttling here and there, wielding brooms and shovels. The white and red Danish flag is very festive. The sun was out now and the place was certainly looking gay.

Robin's friends lived in the last house in town. It was a long way past the store and down the far side into what must have been the original settlement.

"Oh I forgot to tell you," said Robin as we followed him along. "Do you know why that man told us not to camp round by the mine?"

"No," I said intrigued.

"It's radioactive," he answered.

"Good Heavens!" I exclaimed horrified. "Throw away all those stones with crystals in we've got back at the camp."

Robin was first up the outside staircase into the little house. A pretty girl was sitting, eating a huge plateful of black meat. A lidless basin was bubbling away on the hearth. I looked closely to identify the meat: a black nose with whiskers and the remains of a silky skin. It must have been the seal we saw in the market. Robin's friend was ladling out huge platefuls for Robin and Hugh. I felt I couldn't face it as the time was not yet 9 a.m. I sat in the next room, among plastic Jesuses and plants and pictures. A woman was fast asleep on the sofa, her two children on the floor. This would have looked perfectly normal in a genuine Eskimo house with a sleeping shelf but here in this trim, Danish, suburban one it seemed slightly incongruous. A newly shot eagle's foot was the centrepiece of the table.

The Queen was due at 10 a.m. but there seemed to be no hurry. People wandered in and out, chewing pieces of meat and borrowing odd socks or a comb or for a look in the mirror. Then we set off. Everyone walking in the same direction, speeding up as we approached the rise looking down to the harbour. We just topped it to see the most magnificent boat steaming towards us. It was small and squat, yet incredibly regal. The prow was of the Golden Hind type, gilded and gleaming. A mass of people were collecting on the shore, many in Eskimo beadwork clothes. But often these were on pale interbred women and children, as if trying to prove they were genuine Eskimo. Rory ran past me with a group of children all armed with red and white flags. There was a gun salute and then I saw the Queen wearing Edinburgh-type tweeds, standing beside her self-conscious prince consort in strict naval uniform. The welcome given by the crowd was genuine enough, but I couldn't help thinking of the 1750s when the trading company inspectors, arrived in the umiaks, travelling in style, swallow-tailed flag, long pipe and silk hat, standing a free binge to the locals.

An ancient old man with a wizened face skidded in his seal skinned kamics and tripped over the rope of the Queen's ship. The Eskimos in the crowd roared with laughter, but the Danish officer on the deck looked slightly put out as he helped the Queen down the gangway. I was worried that she would put her hand on the post at the edge of the jetty. How was she to know that it was still being painted half an hour before? The local council and officials, the best hunters and other dignitaries came forward now to be received. Then, in a colourful mass, the crowd moved back up the hill for the free banquet.

We must forgo the *kafamik* if we were going to move on that day and walked back along the cleaned path towards our camp site, where we fitted the Danish flags to the prow of the canoes and pushed off. I was frightened that the Queen's big ship might start up and tip us over with her wash or, worse still, run us down. We threaded our way through the 'bergs heading for the col on the far side of the fjord. It looked steeper and steeper as we approached. I had dreaded this crossing of the fjord but the distance seemed to be short now that we had Hugh in one canoe and Robin in mine. We moved twice as fast. Rory nestled between my feet and was already asleep, relishing the fact that he was now a passenger and that nobody would ask him to paddle. Rona sat up straight, full of enthusiasm now that she did not have Robin behind her threatening to bump her on the head with his paddle every time she stopped. Looking over my shoulder, I could still see the Queen's ship and the houses of Narssaq but they were quite insignificant on the vast scene. A postage stamp, and quite unimportant. Their world had shrunk, whereas the natural one that we were thankfully back in, completely took over.

There was a strong tide race rushing up the fjord at right angles to our route. But we seemed to cross it with no bother and the shore came down to meet us after only two hours of paddling.

8

HUGH HAD ATTACHED the canoes on the pack frames and helped me to my feet as I put my arms through as if into a rucksack. I hoisted the eighteen-foot long boat across my shoulders and tentatively shuffled one foot in front of the other. The weight was not too great; it was more a matter of balance. We had 1,800 feet to go before topping the col. I carefully felt my way over the shelving rocks but as I gained height shrubs and little bushes became more frequent. They were hanging with luscious fruit but I did not dare stoop down to eat them in case I toppled over. I would have been unable to stand up again without help. I longed to turn round and see the view but that too was impossible. Slowly, inch by inch, I slithered my feet forward and up, and at last the ground began falling away and I had reached the top. I turned round and could see for miles. The sky was clear and the horizon seemed the uppermost part of the world. The Inland Ice came down to meet the sea in great fingers of grey and shades of white. The land was insignificant, small dark patches of rock here and there. Most of the scene was the sea. How can anybody live there at all? I thought. It seemed ridiculous that that very day we had seen well over 300 people and the Danish Queen complete with her retinue.

Gingerly I lowered myself, resting the weight of the canoe on a large boulder. Facing east now, I was looking into a new world. Beyond the placid lochan was the arm of a new fjord. This would lead us to the church at Hvalsey which was where that wedding had taken place in 1408. Going downhill with the canoe on my back was more difficult than going up. I was not tall enough to keep it above the boulders. One end would touch and the whole canoe would swing round throwing me to the ground. I stumbled down and reached the shore of the calm lochan. Thankfully I lowered the canoe off my back straight into the water. Rona had the paddles. She was just a blob in the distance, having walked round the shore. Nothing for it but kneel, like an Indian, in the canoe and paddle with a stick. Geese were gaggling on the slopes to my left. Otherwise there was utter silence. The lochan was shallow and in its peaty coloured water I could see shoals of tiny fish. Colours around me were browns and dark green with a silver light in the sky.

Reaching the far end, I sat on a smooth slab and waited for Hugh. He loaded me up with the canoe again and I set off down a little path. The willow scrub was becoming taller and taller and I had difficulty lifting my load above the sagging branches. I could hear Robin's voice and then noticed a touch of colour below me. He had pitched the tent.

"Dad's going to complain about this site," he shouted at me. "It's very slanty. But there was nothing else for it. When I got here Rory was fast asleep, curled up on top of the rucksack; so I just put the tent on top of him."

Sure enough, the tent was at an odd angle but I was too tired to do anything but make the best of it. Robin already had a fire going and Rona was balancing the billycan precariously on top. Darkness was gathering fast.

"Do you know how far we've come today, Mum?" said Robin. "Already, just in this one afternoon, we've covered more than we usually do in three or four days!"

I sank down beside the fire. Life was easy. For more fuel I only had to stretch out an arm and pull it off the dry shrubs all round. Hugh produced a bottle of rum that he had been secretly carrying. I poured a good swig into my mug of tea.

"Look at that," said Rona pointing to the now inky black sky. A bright star was moving fast across. A meteorite? Man-made satellite? We never knew. I was reluctant to crawl into my slanting bed, so protracted the evening by sitting round the fire. Hugh, though, had still two nights' sleep to make up and urged us to bed. I was so tired that it was easier to stay where I was than to make the effort to move.

I woke in the early hours of the morning to the sound of rain. No one else stirred. I crawled out of the bag to pitch the fly sheet. Already our belongings, scattered around the tent in an untidy way, were wet. The thin material of the fly sheet was old and rotten so had to be handled with great care. I threw it across the tent then realized that I couldn't pitch it because Robin's camp site incorporated a large slab of rock at the door. I crawled back to bed and pretended I did not know that it was raining.

There was no wind and the low mist in the morning accentuated the placidness of our surroundings. The harsh, rugged mountain tops were veiled, only the lower green slopes were visible.

We loaded up and pushed our way downhill through the willow scrub. Over a little rise and there below me was the sea. Forgetting my load I moved too quickly and found myself hanging, with the canoe balanced between two shrubs and my feet flailing the air.

"Look at Mum," shouted Rory, laughing.

The stream from the little lochan entered the sea below us, forming a gentle bank of macha. Between me and it, though, was a thick alder forest of three or four feet high. As difficult to walk through as the rain forests of South America.

At last we had the canoe loaded and launched and we slipped into the water. Our destination now was across this fjord and down the far coast to our next portage. It was absolutely calm and we paddled across at a fast speed. Now we could really cover the map. Robin and I, both paddling at once, could move our canoe at the speed of about five miles per hour. Quite different from the situation when it was just my arms versus the sea. We were soon across and paddling close to the shore of steep white rock, forming ledges below the water. Swarms of fish lay motionless above each other on the rock shelves. A secret bay opened up into a clachan. The whole scene in fact, was very like the outer isles of the west of Scotland. There was no ice. The water was greener. The tide unimportant.

"A Viking house," shouted Rona already ashore. No wonder, I thought. What a glorious place and how I would love to have had the chance to settle here.

Only when I stepped out of the canoe did I realize that I was saturated. The rain had found its way into all the joins in my

Robin brings cod from the fjord for supper

Two Scots and five Scraelings

Rounding SW. cape between Eric's fjord and Igaliko: Myrtle, Robin and Rory

Viking storehouse—"fortification" on map—Igaliko fjord

Myrtle with Eskimo friend fixing canoes on to carrier,
Igaliko settlement

Family camp at Eric's fjord

At Igaliko
settlement

Below:
Igaliko fjord

Rona

Below left: Robin

Below: Rory

clothes and the wetness now squelched out of the bottom of my trousers as I tried to move up the shingle beach. It was still raining.

"No point in stopping yet," said Hugh. "We might as well push on, seeing as how we're so wet already. A small walk leads us to another little lochan. Let's do that and then stop for lunch."

"Look at the berries," cried Rory.

Already Rona was crouched on the grass picking the juicy purple blaeberries with both hands at once.

The grass had grown thickly on the walls of the Viking house. The place felt settled; quite different from others I had visited farther north, where one had the impression of raw, virgin soil. Here, on the other hand, I felt that people had lived and died; in fact, that the Vikings were still here. Yet the atmosphere was friendly.

The Vikings believed that an unhappy ghost would walk around the area where he had lived and one of these "walkers after death" was considered terrible and dangerous and the only course open to the relatives to deal with the situation was to break open the grave and kill the body a second time. Archaeologists believe that this is the reason why so many of the early graves in Europe, as well as those at Erik the Red's site, were broken into. The Vikings tried to prevent this happening by keeping the dead happy. It was their responsibility to maintain the grave and keep its surroundings in good order so the departed would never feel forsaken. If the body had been buried at sea or had died far away from his home they would put up a stone in his memory at the place where he really belonged. The arrival of Christianity in Greenland had upset the old custom of burying a man where he died. The new belief emphasized the importance of consecrated ground. So to go along with this idea they drove a stake into the ground above the dead person's breast and later, when the priest arrived, the stake would be pulled out and holy water poured down the hole and funeral rites performed, however long after the burial it might be. The Christians were as frightened of a walking ghost as the heathens had been. They forbade the practice of cremation and required a simple earth grave facing east to west without any goods or chattels.

Holding a strong grip on the mind and spirit of the Vikings, pagan or Christian, was the notion of the family. The family unit was indispensable in death as well as life, and every man was absolutely responsible for his offspring. They believed that the man's life and character began with his ancestors; through the generations there was a constant thread and no man could escape the fact that he had inherited both the good and the bad of his father.

Robin interrupted my thoughts. "I've taken one load already, Mum. Aren't you going to carry anything? It's no distance."

I picked up an armful of bags and squelched through the rain. Sure enough it was only about five minutes' walk to the shore of a small stretch of water. Beyond it the ground fell away gently leading down to the sea.

"Let's push on down to the shore," I said. "I can't face the thought of stopping here drying off and having to get going again."

Carrying our loads we walked down to the shore. This finger of the fjord was more like a Scottish loch than the open sea. There was no evidence of waves or feeling of the vastness of the ocean. The smell, though, was genuine enough. Decaying seaweed! A crown of mosquitoes hovered over the rotting heaps. There were so many of them I could actually feel their pressure against my legs as I walked through. Hugh pitched the tent at the very edge of the land. Once inside out of the rain, I realized that the softness underneath us was in fact the seaweed. The groundsheet might keep the dampness out, but not the smell. The primus tottered on the unstable ground, as I stirred in the kidney soup.

"Ugh!" said Rona, "that looks exactly like the seaweed. Absolutely revolting."

The heat of the primus turned our wet soggy clothes into steam. The atmosphere in the tent was like a sauna. My wet clothes clung to me. I would either have to take the whole lot off now or get moving again quickly.

"I couldn't bear to spend the night here," I said in a petulant voice. "This stink is absolutely frightful. Let's push on."

To my surprise everyone agreed. I remembered that on the bottom of my rucksack I had some nylon shopping bags that I had brought specially to beat the mosquitoes. So far we had never had to use them. I dug them out now and Rona and Rory immediately pulled one over their heads peering out through the close woven net like bank robbers.

We pushed off into the flat calm, the rain beating down even the merest ripple. The mountains and rocks and sparseness of Greenland were still masked by the low mist, leaving only the gentle strip of green along the shore visible. There were ruins everywhere. We could see the dark green of the lush vegetation growing over the sites. We crossed another arm of the fjord towards the lower reaches of the steep cliff. A little shingle bay of white pebbles nestled at its foot. The place looked clean and well washed. No seaweed or midges.

"Let's halt there," I shouted across to Hugh. "That looks just marvellous."

Steep shingle makes the best landing for the canoes. Sideways on, one can jump ashore without grounding the boat. Then it's easy to pull it up behind and lift it straight out of the water, above high tide mark. Rock slabs rose above the shingle bay and above this a ledge of green. An ideal camp site, absolutely level and so even Hugh could not complain. There was just room for the guy ropes between the rocks and a slightly higher ledge for our fire. The rain had stopped now and the clouds crept back a little, exposing more Viking ruins on all the available level places about us.

"There must have been thousands of these Vikings," I said to Hugh. "Every single place where you could have built a house that we have seen, had one. Whatever do you think happened? I have a feeling there were just too many of them. Do you think that's true?"

"I think you're right," said Hugh. "Travelling close to the land like this we know that the soil is thin and even now, in late August, the grass from which the people could make their hay is only a few inches long. These Vikings were just too big for the environment.

"Tall people have no real place in the Arctic. They are

dionosaurs. They eat too much, lose too much heat to the cold and take up more space in a tent or house. It is then more difficult to heat. The Eskimos, even after 20,000 years of evolution, are small, intelligent people whose centre of gravity in the kayak is low. The same food would feed four Eskimos but only three Vikings."

"Yes, you're right," I said, "it's the same with us. I'm so glad that our children are small. I hate it when they bring a friend camping with us and their legs stick out of the tent."

"Yes," agreed Hugh. "This was an elementary fact that Captain Scott failed to appreciate on his journey to the South Pole. Big men require more food and they die first on equal but inadequate rations. He should have given his big men far more to eat than the smaller, more compact people. People tend to think that the big he-men, the strong heavy-weight athletes, are the best people for an expedition, but this is just not true."

"Let's have some rum," I interrupted.

"In the Arctic," continued Hugh, "the smallest form of life, the insects, living close or in the tundra, are among the most successful."

With his mind on what he was saying rather than doing, Hugh poured me out a stiff quantity of rum into my plastic mug of tea. Robin held his out and Hugh gave him some too. I was glad to see that Hugh did this without question. After so many weeks of being the man on the expedition Robin was now demoted to being a boy. It was difficult for him and I could feel the rivalry between him and his father. It is difficult to go back down the pecking order once you have been at the top. The fact was, of course, I'd really needed Robin and I had leant on him to fill the gaps of Hugh's absence. Hugh was in the difficult position of joining a close-knit community; rather the same problem as arriving at a party stone cold sober when everybody else is drunk. And then trying to join the crowd.

"I think," said Hugh, "that the Vikings had a population explosion and the arable land ran out, the sons having to move on to increasingly poorer pastures. Just look at it round here.

The oldest ruins are the ones nearest the sea, but up on more marginal strips of grass, like the strip we're on now, the buildings are more recent. The graves from the last stages of the Viking settlement contained people who were stunted and twisted, not from evolution, as is sometimes said, but, I'm quite sure, from starvation."

I agreed with Hugh. Our evidence had certainly proved this point. Now that we were getting closer and closer to the centre of the Viking settlements at the church at Hvalsey, there was more and more evidence of a large quantity of people living on this very small strip of land between the mountains and the sea.

The Vikings were tied to their agricultural economy. They had never adapted to the nomadic ways of the Eskimos whose food gathering was over an enormous stretch of land rather than a small, intensively cultivated patch.

"The Vikings' way was completely geared to the land," said Hugh in a considered tone. "There was no insurance against a bad hay crop due to a cold summer or early frost. According to some archaeologists a plague of caterpillars descended on the area in about 1710, and there was no margin for this sort of thing when every blade of grass had to be counted. On the other hand the Eskimos' insurance was that their harvest of animals, polar bears, seals and reindeer was much less sensitive to small temperature changes. A few degrees could ruin the hay crop and result in no winter fodder for the domestic animals, but the seals would just dive a bit deeper and the reindeer have to scratch a bit more snow off the ground to reach their food. The Eskimos way of life actually thrived on the very difficulties that pushed the Vikings against the wall."

I had to move back from the fire that was scorching my legs. It was dark now but as I turned towards the sea a pillar of yellow light illuminated a circular patch in the inky black scene. The moon was three-quarters full. It appeared to be much closer to us than at home. The oldest stories of the Eskimos have to do with the moon. They noticed that the tide followed the phases and, consequently, it was the moon's spirit that was in control. In early times their word for the moon meant "daylight", perhaps because during the dark part of the year the beams of the moon were far more important than the sun's rays during summer. The light of the moon is actually so strong in Greenland that the full moon can shed much more light than the sun on dull misty days.

The Eskimos have a story of the beginning of the world which is tied in with the moon. It tells of a brother and sister who unfortunately become partners in a game that they called "putting out the lamps". In this, the lights are put out and in the dark the participants sleep with each other. The lights go on and then you must find out who was your partner. Now in the dark, in this story, the girl had marked her partner with soot and when the lamps were lit again she discovered that he was her own brother. Sexual intercourse between such close relatives was absolutely prohibited in Eskimo society. The girl then ran away with a tuft of burning moss in her hand and her brother immediately ran after her. A mad chase followed and the girl fled across the sky. A piece of moss fell and the young man snatched this up and carried it in his hand. As the chase continued the fire in the moss died but the girl was faster than her brother and reached a place higher in the sky. The brother is still trying to catch up with his sister. To the Eskimos, then, the sun is the woman, and it is the moon that is the man. An eclipse of the sun is explained as its journey down to earth when all women must watch out because the sun will get them if she can, being full of jealousy and all the other guiles that are laid at a woman's feet. An eclipse of the moon, on the other hand, is when all men must be careful.

Perhaps, because it is nothing but a woman, the sun does not have a prominent position in Eskimo folklore, whereas the moon is all important. A man lived in it, of course, and he had many functions. His power was vital and important. The Eskimos believed that he sat up there, whittling a walrus tusk so that the chips flew about him and floated down to the earth as snow. It was he that controlled the thunder and lightning, in the same way that he dealt with the rise and fall of the tides; he was also important for the timing of the women's periods and so was responsible for the birth of children. If people broke the various taboos concerned with menstruation or childbirth they had to make it up with the man of the moon. The moon was also a champion of the underdog, a protector of poor people and orphans, and for those who had somehow become desolate and distressed. Because he could work the tides, he was able to control the movements of the animals of the sea—whales, walrus and seals—which were so vitally important to the Eskimos' economy. He could use his power to keep the animals away, as well as being responsible for pushing them ashore.

To the Eskimos there were three powers controlling the world: the air, the sea and the moon. These were omnipresent. The air was everywhere, the sea washed every shore and the moon shone on everything and everybody. The Vikings, on the other hand, considered the sun of paramount importance, perhaps because they knew they would die without it. Like the sun, their chief god, Odin, sat paramount in the sky, in the centre of his great hall, Valhalla, with 600 doors. From his throne he could survey all of creation. He was separated from the earth by a bridge of a trembling rainbow. The flat disc of the earth was surrounded by a great ocean and underneath the disc lay the land of the dead. Looking up now, I thought that the moon had far more influence over our destiny than the sun.

The warmth of the fire, the long day and the rum made me too drowsy to stay upright any more. I snuggled down into the sleeping bag with my head outside the tent. The world was silent and peaceful and I was absolutely content.

We woke to a low mist and calm seas. We were soon off and steaming across the fjord at a fast rate with the wind behind us.

"Look," shouted Robin over his shoulder, "we've already passed that island. That means we've covered seven miles."

I looked at my watch. We had only been going for an hour and a half. We were now approaching the site of Hvalsey. We knew that this was the best preserved church ruin from the mediaeval Norse period in Greenland. From the accounts it was situated at the head of this Qaqortoq fjord, which is divided into two arms by the island that we were now following round its northerly shore. Sited beyond the island, the church would have a fantastic position with a view right down the fjord and out to the open sea.

The mist was rising now and we could see a gently sloping hillside coming up to meet us across the water. The lush slope was bounded towards the north by a belt of rocks. As we paddled along I reminded Robin of the last wedding to be held in the church that we would soon find. The couple had come from farms in the area and had been married in the church packed with friends and relations. It was autumn, so perhaps the hay had been gathered in and the people were meeting together to celebrate the fact that the summer's work was over, as well as the wedding of the two young people. Weddings didn't often happen during the summer, when everyone was hard at work filling up the storehouses and barns with hay, sorting fish, skins for clothes and barter, and making the sour milk. The surroundings seemed benign enough. What then had killed off the bride and groom, to say nothing of the congregation?

Sure enough, sudden death from disease or accident must have been frequent. However charming to the eye, the Greenland landscape and weather were ruthless, not to mention the sea. Shipwrecks were common and the voyages either back to Iceland or across to the New World were long and dangerous. That many people did die at sea has been proved by the finding of "runic staffs". The body would be given a sea burial, but later the family would go through the motions of a funeral and place a wooden pole above the grave bearing the inscription of whom the grave belonged to and often something about where and when he had died.

One wooden runic inscription from a grave revealed more about the dead owner than many others. The wooden stick was found in the corner of a coffin in a graveyard to the north of where we now were. The inscription read "This woman whose name was Gudveig, was committed to the deep in the Greenland Sea". She had died on her way to Greenland and, without the blessing of the new Christian Church, her body had been given a sea burial. As she had not been buried in consecrated ground how could she be saved from the devil? Her husband would be anxious for her salvation and the only course left to him was to cling to the old idea of the identity between a person and the name. The runic staff achieved the equivalent of burial in consecrated ground because the name "Gudveig" was as important as her bones. Heathen notions like this lived on alongside Christian ones long after the people had accepted the new beliefs.

I felt the presence of the church, then I saw it: set back on a grassy meadow, lichen covered, grey on pinkish sandstone. There were buttercups dotted about. It was part of the environment, part of the scene. There was no intrusion, no feeling that man had left his fingerprint. It was almost exactly a thousand years ago since Erik the Red's cousin had settled here. We all paddled fast, wanting to arrive. The onshore wind helped us and soon we were pulling the canoes up onto the shingle shore. A steep mud bank and then we stood looking at the rectangular church of carefully laid stones.

"Rory," I said. "You do know, don't you, that this is why we've come to Greenland?"

"What do you mean, Mum?"

"Well, this is the last reliable written mention of the Norsemen. The letter, I mean, telling about it. It was written from this very place."

"Look at the size of those blocks," said Robin. "It would take at least five men to lift them."

He was pointing to the huge stones forming the lower part of the walls.

"I can see the lime mortar that jointed them together," said Hugh, walking towards the building.

I felt a strange reluctance, an intrusion. I didn't really want to go any closer. The straight lines of the wall were now softened by the movements of Rory and Rona as they moved around and peered into the nooks and crannies between the stone walls. The only sounds were of the sea—a gentle lapping—and twitterings of the wheatears which were pottering around on top of the ruin. The sky was absolutely blue, with touches here and there of mist.

The soil was so thin, scuffing with my foot I was soon down to bedrock. Were there just too many of them then? Is that why they died? Was it just because they did not have the mobility of the Eskimos and needed more and more space for their cows and sheep? Did they ask too much of their surroundings? For 500 years the people were here, seventeen generations or so. They had only sheepskin with which to keep warm, no firearms. I looked again at the church. Its stark simplicity appealed to me. There was no ornamentation, no buttresses or flying angels. It was very Norse. A raven flew out from the walls. It gave its harsh call. It seemed to me at that moment that it was far more in keeping than, for instance, a nightingale at Chartres. No velvet and trappings and beautiful figures to divert our attention.

"Come on, Mum," shouted Rory. "Aren't you coming to see?"

I followed them across the meadow. This Hvalsey church had been so well preserved because the stones were laid in lime. Most of the other mediaeval ones were built of stones placed directly in layers of clay with the joints secured after the walls had been built. In this one, however, the dry stones had been put into lime mortar so that when the roof went the mortar, being waterproof, held the stones in position. In others the clay became rain soaked, allowing the stones to slide. The walls here were complete. The window on the far, or northern, wall was topped by a segmental arch, a type not common in Scandinavia until after 1300 and can only have come to Greenland from there. It was made with such excellent workmanship that it was apparently the only one of its kind for more than six centuries.

"Do you see, it's a double square?" shouted Hugh, who had been pacing along the outer perimeter.

"What do you mean by that?" I asked.

"Well, it's about sixteen metres long and just over eight and a half wide at the broadest point."

"What do you mean by that?" I said. "I don't understand metres."

"Well look, Mum," explained Robin. "The walls are about three and a half metres high, so you can see how high that is, about twice the height of me."

The west gable wall contained a square door and, higher up, a window. The church must have had a pitched roof, the floor-to-ceiling height at the top of the pitch being just over seven metres. With this size, at least 30 or 35 worshippers could have found room inside.

"Do you think they had glass in the windows?" asked Rona.

"Quite possibly," I said, "because at Gardar, which we haven't reached yet, a piece of opaque greenish glass was found; and we also know that window panes were sometimes used by the Vikings in churches in Scandinavia at this time. So I think there could well have been."

"Gosh," said Rory, "look at that. Have you looked at this, everybody?"

He was standing in the doorway pointing to the huge long lintel post above it and supporting the weight of the upper wall.

"Oh look," he said, his attention changing, "something's been in here. Look at that pile of manure. What do you think it was?"

"Sheep, of course," I said, "and what a shame. Look at the damage they did when they got inside our fence at home. Remember when you left the gate open? In about half an hour they had trampled down those new trees we had planted and broken down a wall. The church might have stood the ravages of 300 years, the frost and snow, but it wouldn't stand the sheep for much longer."

"Look what I've found," shrieked Rona, with excitement.

She had been peering into a crack below where the huge lintel joined a smaller stone. I rushed over. Was it a runic inscription? What treasure had she found?

"Oh Rona," said Robin with disappointment, "it's only a nest."

"But it's got an egg in it," she said, fiddling with her fingers and pulling out a tiny little fragile shell of blue. The children were enchanted, far more excited with their find than Norse ruins and Viking graves.

"Why were there two doors on that side facing the sea?" I said to Hugh. "Why do you think they needed two? There can't have been so much of a rush to get in and out that it would need three separate entrances."

I was standing inside the church, looking out. The scene was framed by the old walls. At least the sea, the sun and the birds haven't changed in 500 years, I thought.

"Mum, Mum," it was Rory. He had run in and was dragging at me. "Quick, come," he shouted in a stage whisper. "Look, look."

He beckoned me to the door and to crouch down. We peeped out and he pointed to a chocolate-coloured rock on a ledge slightly higher up on the rock outcrop behind the church.

"Well," I said.

"It's a dog," said Rory. "Look."

Just then the chocolate rock unfolded. A cheeky little face with two quizzing black eyes peeped down at us. It was a fox cub. It stood up now on long spindly legs, stretched and yawned. It was no bigger than a terrier pup. Then another one stood up behind it. It had not seen us and was completely unperturbed. They looked around.

"I know," I said, "they're waiting for their mother."

Out of the corner of my eye I had detected a movement. A small female fox was scurrying from boulder to boulder trying to circle round us and return to her cubs. I pulled Rory down into the church, to give her a chance. But Robin and Rona were still outside. They were jumping off tumbled stones from another building. The fox saw then and skedaddled back into cover. The baby foxes now barked. They were hungry.

"Whatever will they eat?" said Rona, looking around the empty hillside.

"Foxes can fast for long periods," I answered, "but I've never seen one that wasn't absolutely famished. I've seen them hanging around stretches of open water during the winter on the ice. There, constantly moving up and down, you'll see foxes patiently waiting for something edible to appear. Often this is the only movement in the whole scene during the winter and the foxes are usually rewarded for their patience. You often see bears hanging around such places too, but they never seem to catch anything and often go away far hungrier than the fox. All that these foxes will eat, though, are the baby wheatears, I think."

"And the droppings from the sheep," joined in Hugh. "There's something very special about these foxes," he added. "They have the soles of their feet covered with hairs. They can make these hairs stand erect too, and in this way they are able to double the insulation and so keep their feet warm in the depth of winter."

"Look at its sweet face," said Rona. "It hasn't got the foxy look of the ones we see at home."

Rona was right. The Arctic fox has a much more rounded head and its ears are far shorter than the long ones of the red fox with his slender pointed face. This tendency to reduce projecting body parts is general among Arctic animals. The musk ox, for instance, is compact and heavy, its tail extremely short, its legs stout and its neck thick and broad, as well as having a round face with tiny ears almost concealed in its fur. It is the same with the lemmings, hares and also the bears and deer. The fox, however, is the most easy comparison with which to prove this point. Consider the desert fox with enormous pointed ears, snout and tail. It encounters difficulties exactly opposite to its cousin the Arctic fox and so its body surface is increased drastically in order to facilitate dispersing the extra heat as much as possible.

"Look at the fox now," shouted Rory. "It's eating the berries."

Sure enough, it kept putting its muzzle down into the small creeping shrubs and snatching up mouthfuls of black juicy fruit. Like the Eskimos it seemed to prefer the small, black crow berries to the ones we liked most, the blaeberries. They seemed to us better flavoured, more juicy and sweet. But the Eskimos believe they are the cause of dental decay. They collect masses and masses of the black crow berries; but what they consider a real delicacy are the cloud berries. They like to eat them served in a mixture of seal oil and chewed caribou fat which is beaten up until it is frothy and looks rather like ice cream.

"Come over here," shouted Robin, "there is a very complicated house."

We could only see the top of his head. He was obviously inside the sunken interior, hidden from us by turf-clad walls. A long roofless corridor led from close by the church to where Robin was standing. The doorway of the house was still intact. Standing on the lintel above this doorway I could see that there were many buildings and rooms radiating out from this central point. Robin clambered up to stand beside me.

"Why is this house so different from the others we've seen, do you think?" he asked. "It isn't that this place looks particularly lush or anything like that, to need such a complicated mass of buildings."

"Well," I answered, "the archaeologists seem to think that a climatic change occurred some time towards the end of the thirteenth century when the average temperature dropped considerably. This change is believed to be the cause of the alteration in the building technique.

"In the early days the main concern of the settlers was to place their byres in the best place for retaining the heat. Cows are very difficult to house, and the early settlers couldn't replace them, so they just had to survive the winter. To do this they must be protected against the cold. When new buildings were erected to replace original ones the settlers had thrown up quickly before the onslaught of that first winter, they paid great attention to this fact. And, as the years went by, they seemed to have had to take more and more care of the animals. Instead of the original detached dwelling houses and byres, like the ones we saw at Erik the Red's farm, they seemed to have all the rooms together in one single block of buildings with the central one, which would naturally be the most sheltered and the warmest, reserved for the cows. This type of farm was called centralized and is only found in Greenland."

"How on earth did they roof all those straggling buildings?" asked Robin.

"I think," I said, "that each one must have had its roof and then the whole lot would be covered with turf so that from the outside a house would more or less disappear into the scenery. They must have been terribly damp. Water from the roof must have seeped down into the walls and then run along the ground. It couldn't have disappeared because of the permafrost. The houses would be practically impossible to air but they must, all the same, have been just the answer to retaining the heat. Nowadays we think about double glazing. Well, the Vikings got round that difficulty by having no windows. No air could get in but, on the other hand of course, no warm air would escape."

"It must have been a constant job keeping these houses in condition," said Hugh. "Just mere homesteading must have occupied a fantastic amount of the men's time. You need a great deal of energy and vigour for that sort of thing and I think that proves that this was not a stagnant or disintegrating society. At this time the people living in these buildings, constructing this type of settlement, would have been here for perhaps the third generation. The settlers' existence would be confined to the areas round and about here, and was based on the raising of cattle and sheep, on hunting, and then perhaps on one daring trip to visit settlers in other parts of Greenland. Their chance of reaching further than the Greenland shores was negligible. Perhaps a few adventurous sailors would go off to make their way to Norway or head out in the other direction. They probably were prompted to set off by the settlers' need for long beams of wood for making the roof that we were talking about a minute ago. That was one thing that the settlers needed from further afield."

While Hugh was speaking my eyes slowly swept the surroundings. These farm buildings were in no way monumental. The turf walls now blended the ruins into the surrounding landscape. The scene must have been very similar in the days when the houses were occupied. The only building to catch the eye in those days, as now, would be the church with its grey stone wall. Yet even that was not particularly conspicuous. From here the wall could easily be mistaken for rock, thrusting itself through the green soil. There was a great charm and enchantment to this place in the August air. The sun shone brightly, the sky was clear and the air dry, yet not too hot. There were berries to pick and plenty of fuel and fjord stuffed with fish.

"What do you think the children did all day?" asked Rona.

"That's easy," I said, "they'd have to work. There wouldn't be much time for playing in August when the families would know that the winter was ready to creep up on them at any time. The main thing they would have to do would be collect fuel for the winter. They'd go out to collect the twigs and stems of the willow, the dwarf birch, junipers and all those shrubs that the berries grow on. They would then have to carry them back to the farms, heaping them together in enormous bundles and carrying them on their backs."

"Supposing they hurt themselves," interrupted Rory.

"They knew quite a bit about medicine," answered Hugh. "These Vikings had to develop some skill in the treatment of injuries."

"Yes," I said, "I remember reading a story about the death of the great leader, Thormod. He was mortally wounded in a battle in 1030. He pulled an arrow out of his chest and looked at the bits of flesh sticking to the barb, saying 'I still have fat round the roots of my heart'. The story went on to give a description of the ways in which the wounded were treated after this particular battle. The men were carried off to nearby barns, where women heated water and dressed the wounds. Then they prepared a porridge made of onions, which the wounded men were made to eat. If the smell of onions then came from the wound in the man's stomach it proved that his intestines had been pierced, which, in those days, would mean death. This explains Thormod's other remark that is quoted in the story. When he was offered this porridge he said 'Take it away, I am not suffering from the onion illness'. He knew that his wound was not in his stomach but in his heart."

During the time we had spent at Hvalsey a strong wind had blown up and looking out to sea I realized we would have a struggle to beat the waves now slashing against the shore.

"We'd better go now," I said to Hugh, "or we'll never get away."

We ran back through the meadow down to the water's edge. Spray was being thrown up and wetting us as we stood in the sparkling sun.

"The kids will have to walk," said Hugh. "Go along the shore and we'll pick you up at the head of the fjord. Come on, hurry up. You get in first and I'll give you a shove off."

We lifted the canoe into the water and I waded out to knee depth before stepping quickly over the side and sitting down before the canoe was whipped round by the waves and tipped. Using all my strength, I just made headway and managed to get beyond the breakers. Now I had to turn parallel to the shore. Waves broke into the cockpit, sousing me with cold water. But I was round. I was only a few yards off shore but even so there were white horses between me and the beach. In spite of the winds we easily outdistanced the children.

"Round that point," I yelled to Hugh, "we're bound to be sheltered there."

He could not hear me and my face was wet with spray when I tried to turn to shout again. He drew ahead of me. When I saw how his canoe tossed and turned in the water I realized that mine must be doing the same. Only the width and length of our craft enabled us to beat the waves.

Rounding the point, and now at the very head of the fjord, we were absolutely at the mercy of the onshore wind. I clutched a rock and attempted to fend-off the canoe, waiting for the children to arrive. My arms were not strong enough and I realized that I would be swept onto the rocks and beaten by the weight of the waves. Nothing for it but to push off and stand further out in the bay. The canoe rose and fell like a cork. Stationary, I suddenly felt seasick. Just then the bright red cagouls of the children appeared over a rise in the ground. I paddled back to the shore.

"Quick, quick," I yelled at Robin. "You have to leap in in one go when I come close. If I stop I'll get battered against the rocks." He clutched Rory by the hand and dragged him quickly down to the water's edge.

"I'll throw him in," he shouted to me.

I came as close as I could and just as Robin lifted Rory off his feet he began to shout and flay his legs.

"I've forgotten my nest," he yelled, "I'll have to go back for it. You've got to wait." Shouting and protesting loudly Robin threw him towards me. I nearly overbalanced when Rory's weight hit the side of the canoe. I clutched him by his anorak and managed to throw him down onto the deck. Robin followed with a thud and I just managed to get us away from the rocks. I could not turn round to see how the others had fared.

"Paddle, paddle," I yelled at Robin. We were just about to be thrown up on the beach when, with both of us using all our strength, we managed to turn and head back into the waves. "We've got to cross that estuary," I shouted to Robin. "We'll camp once we are beyond it. There's absolutely no shelter on this side."

"I wish we had a nice turf house to get into out of the wind."

I could not think in the wind. It was an evil, battering thing, hammering any sense out of my mind. It was tearing at my hair, throwing the sea at us in a fury. I could imagine why the Vikings believed in the horrors that lurked in the deep.

We beat the wind and in a few minutes had reached the shelter on the lee shore.

"I can't go much further," I shouted to Hugh who now drew alongside us.

I pointed to a ledge above a sandy beach ahead. He overtook us, pulled up his canoe and signalled to us that the site was suitable. I was cold and wet from the spray. I was so stiff I wondered how I could possibly clamber out of the canoe. Robin, in better shape than me, beached the canoe and helped me out. I staggered up the grassy bank to where Hugh was already battling with the flapping canvas. As I stood and watched him I became aware that water was seeping up around my feet. Then I realized that it was flowing!

"We can't camp here," I said to him indignantly, "it's on a stream bed."

"Why not?" he said, "all the best bedrooms have running water. Let's have a tot of rum for all crew."

"Have you seen the berries?" shouted Rona. "They're the best yet, absolutely enormous." She came up with a handful of fruit about the size of a small plum.

Hugh now had won the fight with the wind and the tent was up. Thankfully I crawled in.

"We'll have to do something about the floor," I said, "it'll be freezing with all this water just below the groundsheet."

"I've got the very thing," he answered, opening his briefcase and pulling out a thick wad of papers. He carefully laid these out and we lay down on the *Journal of Chronobiology*.

9

We started off from the damp soggy, camp site early in the morning. We now had to travel down the fjord before we could round the corner into Igaliko Fjord. Our first difficulty was to traverse the big bay that would take us half way down the island situated in the middle of the fjord. There would be no shelter from the strong wind for many miles. The shortest way was far out, but I was reluctant to cut our umbilical cord with the shore.

"Wind's rising," said Robin. "We'll have to hurry up, Mum."

I knew he was right and realized that if we were going to cover the distance we must draw further off shore. Hugh and Rona were far out on our right. An hour went by. We could now see the glaciated slabs of the far side. The wind was on our cheeks and not full against our faces. This spurred me on and Robin and I soon drew away from the others and reached the most perfect harbour between the rocks. Seaweed rose and fell gently beneath us and, looking carefully, we could see shoals of fish lying on the rocky ledges. The island looked bleak and inhospitable yet I could make out the unmistakable lushness in the centre of the valley opposite us. A Viking family must have lived there. How did they put up with the wind?

We now had to round the point. Gingerly we pushed off again when the others had caught us up. Our route ahead looked blocked by an enormous wall of white, but as we crept further round I saw that it was a floating 'berg. The biggest yet! It was a towering castle, with more flanking it on either side and others beyond. The wind was now on our shoulders and I knew that if we could only make the distance it would soon turn and be on our backs. Time passed. Our minds were only considering the making of the distance. I paddled mechanically, keeping going by concentrating on the shape and colour and size of the icebergs as we drew alongside and then past them. To look far ahead was too soul-destroying. The distances, now that we were out, away from the shelter of the island, was so vast that one became overwhelmed. Another hour passed.

"Mum," said Robin turning round. "Do you realize?"

"What?" I said. "What are you talking about?"

"Do you realize the wind is on our backs. Can't you see the waves. They're going with us." He was right and now the land was falling back into Igaliko Fjord.

I had a great feeling of achievement as we rounded the final spur of rock. I couldn't resist shouting out. Robin began to sing. We roared out the words together. Quite inappropriately we sang "Now the Carnival is Over, It is time to say goodbye". For the first time that day our words were not thrown back into our faces. The rollers were picking us up and whisking us along. The following waves would come into view in the corner of my eye. I would feel them underneath the canoe. The front would tip up and then they were gone, leaving us trailing behind in their wake. The shore was rushing past at a fast speed. I was tired, but no question of stopping now. The tide as well as the waves were in our favour. Glancing round I glimpsed water. A wave at eye level, going in the same direction. The whole Atlantic seemed to be whirling into our fjord. We were planeing on the waves, with the sea picking us up and sweeping us along.

I knew from the map that an inlet should be coming up on our left, when I saw the rocks and steep cliffs fall back. Suddenly it was calm and peaceful. We paddled in towards a green place above the grey rocks. It was so marvellous to be out of the wind. I pushed my anorak hood back and for the first time really looked around.

"Eskimo ruins," pointed Robin, as we drew near to the shore. A round circle of stones denoted an old site. "New or old?" he asked.

We scrambled ashore and I found that when I lifted one of the grey boulders the tundra had grown at least three inches above its impression. It must have been perhaps 300 years since anyone had camped here. Hugh began to gather wood.

"I'm going to pitch the tent tonight," I said definitely. "No more of your wet-sog sites."

My decision was easy. The Eskimos had chosen the most ideal place. It was absolutely level and soft, and once we had kicked the boulders further out, as our tent occupied more space than theirs, there was the perfect site for us for the night. That'll confuse the archaeologists, again I thought, as I removed yet another of the stones.

Robin still had energy left to fish. The bay that we were in certainly looked ideal. We knew that a small burn entered it at its head with a lochan above. Obviously a good place at this time of the year when the salmon were beginning to run into fresh water to spawn. I crawled into the tent to lay out the sleeping bag and consider what we should have for tea.

"Help me," yelled Robin. He sounded as if he really needed it. Hastily I poked my head out. "Help," he shouted again, "I've caught a shark." I looked around for Hugh. No sign.

"Hang on to the line," I yelled thinking that there would be enough food on it for many days ahead.

"Help," Robin yelled again and then I realized that his canoe was moving out to sea, and he wasn't paddling. The shark had caught him! A large black shape rose to the surface, a triangular fin, the canoe picked up speed and began to move sideways on, turning this way and that as the huge fish tried to throw itself free.

"Drop the line," I cried, but that was the one thing Robin had no intention of doing. Then suddenly it was gone, hooks and all. Crestfallen, Robin picked up the paddle and returned to the shore.

"There's something very odd across the other side of the bay," said Hugh as he returned with an armful of driftwood. "It's a huge rock and on top there is also a building. I can't think what on earth it is."

"I'm too tired to be the least bit interested in the Vikings," I said petulantly, "and we haven't got any food. Somebody will have to go and catch something edible, instead of just fooling around with a shark." Hugh took Robin's place in the canoe. Five minutes later he was back, having caught four. Three were cod with their black body lining but the fourth was different. It was an Arctic char. As Hugh gutted it, the beautiful fatty yellow flesh made my mouth water as I heated up the frying pan. Its flesh was far sweeter than the cod and, the best delicacy, frizzed up roe.

We woke the next morning to mist lower than the camp.

"Let's go round to those ruins then," I said. We walked round the silent shore, picking our way over the glaciated rocks with the hummocks and dips of willow scrub.

"Whatever is it, do you think?"

Through the mist I could see a large rock, perhaps ten to fifteen feet high and, perched above, what seemed to be a little house.

"How do you get up?" asked Rory as we drew alongside.

I walked right round and saw that a flight of hewn steps rose from the side facing the sea.

"Perhaps it was a holy place," I said as I climbed up. "No, I think it was a lookout."

I could see farm sites to my left and right with a stream tumbling from the little lochan above. Lapland buntings with splotches of red on their heads and chestnut stripes were chittering about in the willow scrub. A warm hazy sun was now beating the mist.

"I think it was a store," I shouted down to the others. "I'm sure it was because the walls are different from anything we've seen before. This is made with stones carefully placed on top of each other. They don't have any of that binding mortar stuff we've seen before; and do you see how the walls are at their full height? The place is just as it must have been except for the roof."

"Well, why does that make it a store?" shouted up Robin.

"I think they used this method with the specific purpose of airing the place as a storehouse. Heaven knows how they got these boulders up here. They must have used a sort of system of wedges."

I knew that the only method for the preservation of meat

known to the Vikings was drying, and perhaps, now and then, smoking. Salt curing of meat would have been very difficult for them because they could only extract small quantities of the necessary salt from sea water. This would not have produced sufficient. Looking around I realized that this site was a particularly airy place and here the meat would be raised above any marauding foxes. With its dry walls the air could pass freely through the joints and yet the walls were strong enough to discourage any fox that did clamber up the barren piece of rock.

The main diet of the Norsemen was meat, fresh or dried, which they procured by hunting either on dry land or sea. Only sometimes did they use their own domestic animals. Broth was often made from their meat, proved by the vast amount of spoons and ladles that have been found either of bone or wood. They are all of a shape which was characteristic in mediaeval Scandinavia. Everyone had their own spoon, which was even taken along when visiting, carefully kept in a wooden case. The knife with which the meat was cut was kept in the belt in some sort of a leather sheath. Apparently the Christians were caused a lot of trouble by their rules. Since meat formed such an important part of their diet, what were they to do when observing the statutory fasts? In the ecclesiastical section of a *Book of Laws*, printed in Iceland, we can read how they bent the rules. Among the meats which were not to be eaten during times of Lent and so on, were beef, goat, pork, polar bear, reindeer, walrus and seal. The meat of the whale was not mentioned as it was considered a fish, and so could be eaten during these times. In the same way it was permissible to eat web-footed birds, which included hens, whereas talon-footed birds-of-prey, such as falcons and hawks, were forbidden. The eggs of the allowed birds could be eaten only when dairy foods were served. Milk was absolutely prohibited.

All the luxuries had to be imported, which was perhaps the reason for such a large storehouse as this. The people could trade the seal and walrus skins and ivory for sheep and goats as well as corn. The Greenland Vikings were lucky in so far that they could produce various much-coveted articles for which the Europeans would pay handsomely. From the thick skin of the walrus, for instance, a type of heavy rope was made by cutting the skin into long shreds which were then twisted into rope that was so strong that it could be used for the anchoring and mooring of ships. The ivory of the walrus was used instead of the genuine article and so was an even more important export for Greenland. The animal is not found in southern Greenland waters at all, which seems to indicate that either the men from these settlements set off north in their boats or they actually traded with the Eskimos. Annual hunting expeditions in the north are mentioned in some of the earlier Norse literature. The sagas have stanzas telling of nothing but snow, gales and carving icebergs. There is a translation which reads:

> Many men North to the cruel places went,
> Where the Greenland houses end.
> Fishing and hunting there were best,
> For the swift footed hunter's quest.

It is in one of these descriptions of early hunting parties searching for the walrus where the first contact with the Eskimos crops up. In the manuscript it says that "Farther to the North hunters have come across small people, whom they call scraelinga; when they are hit, their wounds turn white and they do not bleed but when they die there is no end of their bleeding. They possess no iron but use walrus tusks for missiles and sharpened stones instead of knives."

The hunters would also have had to travel far to search for the reindeer. They preferred the bow and arrow as a means of killing them, on account of their complete silence. Iron arrow-heads have appeared in great quantities among the finds in the settlements. The settlers brought back the meat either on their backs or on the pack saddles of horses. The remains of saddles have come to light in excavations. There have been no reindeer left in this part of Greenland for many hundreds of years.

I clambered down the hewn steps from the store and thought about the women who must have trudged up and down them, collecting food for the family's meal. The children had wandered away.

"Look at this," said Rona. "I bet that I am in the kitchen. I'm sitting with all sorts of sooty stones around me."

I went over to have a closer look. "No," I said, "I think that is the bathhouse."

She was in a small detached house of one room, of about 2·8 metres by 2·5 and a little depression in one half of the room was occupied by what seemed to be a fire pit. We dug around and found pieces of wood.

"Do you know what?" I said. "I think there would be a bench there. In fact I think I can see a bit of a plank now. Anyway, the bathers would sit on these planks, naked, while water was poured into the fire pit on top of stones which gave off a fantastic amount of steam. They would be gasping in the heat; probably five or six people could sit in a row. This type of bath, which the Scandinavians still love, is called a sauna. Do you remember there's one at the swimming pool at Glasgow."

"Yes," said Rory, "I've seen fat women come running out all red and collapsing into the pool with a great groan and a splash."

"You know," I continued, "there must have been far more wood here in their day."

"Yes," answered Hugh. "Of course they would have a lot of driftwood as we do now, but there would have been far more trees. In fact there would be no shortage of fuel because I have found huge trunks of birch quite far inland; but once they exploited these large tree growths the wind would soon get in, which would tear up the turf and set the light soil drifting over the tundra. This seems to happen all over the world where people begin to fell trees either for cultivating the ground, or burning for fuel. It's still happening. You see it even in the south of England where they're now cutting down their hedges."

We began to wander back along the shore as we spoke.

"Look," said Rory jumping up on top of a flat stone. "Here's another of those fox traps."

"What?" said Hugh, "have you seen those before?"

"Yes," I answered, "we've seen lots of them about. Do you see? They have a sort of passage closed at one end and a trap door at the other. At least that's what I think that flat stone is for. It would fall down and close the passage when the fox had bitten the bait, but I think they would be much more recent than the Vikings, which goes to show perhaps that once they had died out the Eskimos moved in and made the most of the Norsemen's farm sites."

We wandered back to the tent. More fish for lunch, then we were off. We launched the canoes into a stiff breeze and running sea but now we were travelling with it. The wind was on our backs. Ice-swept rocks were on our left-hand side. Nothing to see towards the open fjord on our right as the rollers limited our visibility to a few yards.

"Do you know what?" shouted Hugh. "We're now in the deepest part of the fjord, according to the map. That explains why the waves are so steep."

"Yes," I answered, "but I think they're also meeting the tide which seems to have turned."

We were now being tossed up and down as if passing down rapids in a river. The surface of the sea was thrown up as if rocks were just under the water. I flinched and clutched my paddle expecting the noise of grating, but the canoe sailed on. Obviously there were no rocks below but only the force of the tide and the wind. But now I could see ahead; the water was thrown into a different formation. It was a whirlpool and we were whisked into it before I really had time to think. We shot round and round. I could see out to sea and in the next instant I was looking to the head of the fjord, with the gleam of the Inland Ice above! Then we were round again, round and round, quicker and quicker. I was unable to think, let alone act! But the wind was stronger than the tide and in a few minutes we were cast aside by the whirlpool and left to continue on our way. Terrified of being sucked back again I flayed the water with my paddle.

Ice-smoothed glaciated rocks folded down into the water ahead of us and soon we were into another bay and a perfect harbour. The water was green and completely transparent. I could step out from the canoe onto a dry rock of a silvery colour. Just above was the perfect site for the tent.

"Look," said Robin "that's most peculiar. The beach is above the grass, not below it."

I could see what he meant. "It's a raised beach," I explained. "At one time the sea must have been far, far deeper and all that would have been under the water. If you look, I bet you'll find some fossils and shells. Help me with this boat, though, before you go."

"Look what I've found," shouted Rory.

It wasn't a fossil, but a rusty tin. He brought it up. It was unopened.

"Milk," I said as I wielded the tin opener.

"Oh let me have some," shouted Rona.

"And me," said Robin.

I grabbed the tin back and took a spoonful myself first. Delicious powdered milk. It forms a glutinous mass in your mouth, sticking to your teeth and the roof of your palate, cloying and gelatinous, but absolutely delicious.

"Come and look at this view," shouted Hugh, standing on the raised beach. I joined him on the pile of tiny, completely rounded stones. They must have been tumbled by the ocean for millions of years to have assumed such a perfect matching form. Looking north we had a view to the ice cap with exciting black rock peaks silhouetted against the grey white of the ice. I preferred this bleak ice-type scenery to the more pastoral that we had had round the corner at Hvalsey. I could see Rona and Rory below us sitting on a vast tree trunk. It must have come from Russia, the only source of such wood in the northern hemisphere.

"I think we should stay the night here," said Hugh. "We've got to cross the fjord now, you realize, so that we can get into the fresh water lake."

The lakes to which Hugh was referring were connected to the fjord by a narrow river. They ran parallel northwards, separated from the sea water by a narrow range of low hills. We could see from the map that the upper reaches of the lakes had many small islands. These had seemed to me very typical burial places of the kind that the Vikings seemed to like in Scotland and Denmark. We knew too that the Viking economy was geared to catching salmon. At this time in the early autumn we knew that many of these fish would be swimming from the North Atlantic and now making their way up the streams, rivers and tributaries into their spawning grounds. We felt, from looking at the map, that the lakes would be stuffed with fish. I was keen to visit them too as the scenery would be completely different from what we had experienced so far. Different flowers would grow on a different type of soil. The whole area on the map looked strange and enticing and we all agreed that it would be worth the diversion to make a portage up into them by way of the narrow river and then carry the canoes back down to the sea at the head of the lakes, well to the north.

"Do you think the Vikings went after the salmon then?" asked Rona. "What kind of weapons would they have used if they had met the scraelings over there? We know that Eskimos just love salmon, don't we? Do you remember those ones we saw drying on a string outside the tent at that place where they were collecting the berries?"

"Well," I said, "the Vikings' weapons usually consisted of a sword, an axe, spear and bow and arrow. Of these the ones that they were most proud of were the sword and axe."

"Yes," agreed Hugh, "any self-respecting Viking bore them along with him always."

The Vikings' swords were well known from numerous finds in Scandinavia. They preferred the long broad two-edged iron sword with the hilt made up of four separate pieces. There was the guard, then the flat grip, narrowing away from the blade, another cross piece, called the upper hilt, and finally a triangular pommel. The guards were most commonly straight and the hilt would be inlaid with gold or copper, silver and gilt. The blade itself was often inlaid and the whole sword was a weapon of great splendour. The Vikings indeed loved richness and colour in their weapons and the settlers or "poor relations" living here in Greenland must have hankered after the grandeur of these belongings from home.

"Where did they get these swords from?" said Rona, interrupting my thoughts.

"Well," I answered, "I think they were usually forged outside Scandinavia, in places like France, but we have seen sites of various forges and smithies here in Greenland, and I expect that many of the tools found here prove that they did try to make the blades in Greenland, probably to replace the original ones broken through the years. Apparently the best makers of swords were often the monks, and the Emperor Charlemagne had to bring out a special embargo in the export of weapons, even to the extent of meting out the death penalty for infringement. He drew special attention to the clergy, which suggests that by his time the smithies in the monasteries were more important than those outside. Charlemagne's ban was supposed to keep the weapons away from the blood-thirsty robbers of the north.

"No monasteries, though, made the Vikings' battle axe. To the peoples of western Europe subjected through the ages to the raiding parties of the Vikings, the long handled, broad-edged battle axe became the distinctive symbol of the Viking. 'From the wrath of the Norsemen, oh Lord deliver us,' was a prayer used in the churches of Western Europe in those days."

"They used bows and arrows too," said Rory. "Remember we looked for those arrow heads in the graves we found at first? You told me they had been found alongside the dead in bundles of up to 40."

"Yes," I said, "that was from one of the graves in the west of Greenland but," I added, "the Vikings that came here definitely intended to settle and not to conquer. If you remember the main reason why Erik the Red chose to come back to Greenland was because the land was empty. I think people have been unkind to the Vikings through the years, thinking that they were all blood-thirsty warriors, whereas actually I think they were family people, always looking for somewhere better for their children. Not all out with the idea to steal and raid. It is interesting to think that the Vikings have been and gone and yet that raised beach up there will be here for ever."

I woke up the next morning to the smell of frying. Hugh was already up. I looked out of the tent to a water-colour light of grey and silver. It was 5 am. He was crouching over the fire, making fish cakes. We had never thought of this before. He had mixed last night's cod with the powdered milk. We ate our breakfast, loaded up quickly and pushed off into the flat calm knowing that we would be lucky if it lasted for long. We needed at least three hours to make this long sea crossing. We headed for a point just visible on the far side. Robin and I paddled on and on; on and on. Now at last the cliffs of the far side looked closer than those behind, but would we ever reach them?

"You can make out the stones now," said Robin. "We must be getting close."

Sure enough, by now we could see the regularities in the cliff ahead. Another hour and we were close underneath the towering wall of rock. The water was black and as we rounded the cliff into the long bay of Ekalut the water became darker still. At the head of the bay I knew there was a river but as we approached this point there was no sign of it.

"Must be hidden behind a spit," I said to Robin. He wasn't looking ahead but below.

"Just look at that," he said with excitement. And as I peered into the dark depths I could see bodies of large fish hanging in the water.

"They're salmon," he shouted. "Do you see? They're quite different from the cod."

Rain had started, but we were too excited to care. I could hear the river now and as we drew close to the shore I could just make out where it swirled round the side of a steep sand-bank. We were able to paddle in behind the sand to a secret estuary. It was deep enough for quite a few yards before I urged

Robin to step out of the canoe to lighten it so that I could gain a little more leeway up river.

I was forced out by the shallowness as the water of the river cascaded over a belt of bedrock. We lifted up the gear then carried the canoe over the rock and back into the water again. Robin removed his trousers and waded along behind, pushing the canoe. I walked along the bank carrying the heaviest load.

"I can't bear it any longer, Mum," he said, "my legs are freezing off. You'll have to have a go."

So saying Robin staggered to the shore and splashed out. Gingerly I took off my shoes and trousers and felt the temperature. It was freezing. Nothing for it though but to enter the water. It was better to move the canoes this way than carrying them on our backs. The rain was lashing down now, great sheets of wetness and soon I was as wet above the water as I was below.

"Have to get out now, Mum," shouted Robin, who had drawn ahead and had climbed a little hillock. "There are real rapids with the river falling over a staircase of rocks."

We portaged the canoes the last quarter of a mile and reached at last the fresh-water lake.

The scene was black and gloomy. Rain was driving over the surface in squalls. I was cold.

"Mum," shouted Rory. "Mum, Mum, Mum."

His voice was thrown back from the cliffs on either side of us echoing one from the other.

"For God's sake let's get going," I said to Hugh. "I can't bear it here. Why ever did we come to this darn fresh-water place? It's awful."

"I want my lunch," said Hugh disappointed.

"Oh let's push on," I answered. "Come on."

As I waded back into the water I felt the brush of a large fish against my skin. I screeched.

"The water's stiff with salmon," said Robin peering in. "It seems to be thinner too," he said.

"You're quite right," answered Hugh, "you'll find it much easier to paddle. Salt water makes far more resistance than this."

Dispirited, cold and wet we paddled along the shore that

rose steeply from the water in dark towering shoulders of rock.

After half an hour the lake opened up, and the cliffs gave way to low scrub between tumbled rocks.

"Have to stop for lunch," shouted Hugh over to me. "I can't go any further. I'm just starving."

He turned his canoe and landed ahead of us.

"Look for some wood," he shouted.

"What sort?" I answered. "There's no driftwood here you know."

However, there were quite tall bushes and shrubs of willow and alder with plenty of dead wood among the lower branches. Instead of building a fire Hugh merely struck a match and held it to one of these willows and soon it was blazing up to cheer our spirits.

"Whose going to look for water?" said Rory. "I can't see any streams coming in. This is a daft place to stop."

"Why not use the lake?" I asked him.

"Well, that's one advantage of coming this way, anyway," said Rona.

We sat on the tumbled boulders that had rolled down from the cliffs above and dried off our clothes. Steam rose from my legs. I turned round to do the same to my rear end. The windproof material of my over trousers was far from waterproof but soon I had changed the icy clamminess to a warm cosy sog.

It was difficult to get going again, but soon we could see a belt of rain approaching. This was the moment to be off. Back in the canoe and up our lake, which was widening with every moment in the water. I noticed something black in the sky. As I looked it came lower and lower until a huge bird soared quite close above us masking the sky. There were two of them. No, three! One was much bigger than the others. They swept to one side with the light coming from below. They were eagles. I had never seen anything so exciting. They swooped, then rose and hung in the sky. Another came down to have a look, rising and falling; then the first returned. They became bolder, and lower.

"Look, look," shouted Hugh and I could see he was pointing towards the cliff.

Festoons of sticks were clinging to one spot. It was a nest.

"Hand me the binos," I shouted to Robin who was grovelling between his feet to where I had tossed them in the morning.

I was so excited I could hardly open the case and pull them out. I put the strap round my head and then fixed the lenses in the right direction. A stone was rising from the back of the nest and then I realized it was a fledgling. It was huge, looking like a manikin, peering down.

"It's a hobgoblin," said Rory, suddenly taking notice.

The parent birds were mewing and calling to it, urging it to fly. As we could see the other young was in the sky. The one left ruffled its feathers, moved slightly but remained doggedly on its perch. It was not going to go. I felt for the mother, knowing just the feeling when, in the swimming pool, I have urged the children to jump off the diving board. They teeter on the brink for hours making up their minds. Now the baby eagle opened its mouth. It was huge. Rona and Hugh came alongside.

"We must go up and look," said Hugh in a stage whisper. "We can land here and there is a good place for me to take a photo from."

Sensing our intentions the parent birds swooped lower until I could feel the wind, disturbed by their wings, against my face. We landed, and Rona, Rory and I lay behind a rock gazing up at the nest, perhaps 50 feet above our head.

"I'm coming with you, Dad," said Robin, following Hugh up the steep elbow of the cliff. As we watched they gained height. We saw Robin halt and pick something up. He tossed it in our direction. Rona ran to collect it and brought back a sheep's leg, still with flesh and skin.

I could clearly see the nest made of big pieces of wood. Orange lichen was behind on the red rock with a white perch of guano below. The mother now landed on the far side of the lake and called to her children. The one in the sky came low then landed beside her on a dead tree. The one in the nest, however, called hungrily for food, opening its mouth again and ruffling its shoulders. It seemed oblivious of Hugh and Robin approaching from below. The father, though, was well aware of their intentions. He flew round and round, then swooped. I could feel the might of his body as he came shooting through the air like a jet plane on the attack. Instinctively I put my hands above my head and hid. I could feel Rona and Rory cowering beside me. When we dared look again we could see Robin and Hugh against the ground. They were soon back beside us.

"It's not fair to disturb it," said Hugh. "I'm terrified the baby will fall out of the nest. Come on, let's go."

Both flying above us now, the parent birds made sure that we were leaving. We pushed out into the lake and then there was another swoosh through the air.

"It's coming at us," said Robin, burying his head on his knees.

I felt braver this time and could see that the bird was not actually aiming at us. The weight of its body shot down through the air, smack, into the water. As it rose again it clutched a silvery body in its claws. A salmon. It was not called the Greenland fish eagle for nothing! What a perfect place it had chosen for its nest, unlimited food laid out at its feet.

The rain had now settled in and the wind was tossing the lake into wavelets that were coming and going in a haphazard way all around us. There was no pattern, as in the sea. I saw signs of Vikings on the shore around. But by now the wind was beating on my face and I could feel the strength of it against the paddle. We were very wet and my interest in ruins had abated with the excitement of the eagle. We had now reached the widest part of the odd-shaped lake and here the wind was beating down with full force through a gap in the hills. It was straight off the ice cap; I could feel its chill in my bones.

"This wet cold is what gets one," I said to Robin. "This is the sort of weather in which you'd die of exposure. It's like Scotland. It's the wet cold that gets you, not the real Arctic, where you are always dry. You can stand far worse cold then."

We were growing tired. I wondered if we would, in fact, be able to make the far shore. The lake was black and hostile, and I turned to hug closer to the shore. The trees were the highest yet. Perhaps the Vikings had visited here but they had certainly never lived. This was the type of vegetation that there must have been right along the seaward slopes when they had first arrived. Here the scene looked undisturbed and prehistoric, "as old as unrecorded time" still waiting for man to arrive. The wind was relentless. There was no let-up until, at last, we landed at the furthermost point. We were now faced with a steep portage which would take us back over a col and down towards the sea.

"Real storm coming," said Hugh, "just look at that sky."

There was little of it to see, black clouds were already masking the world in all directions.

"I think we should get over this col though," said Hugh, "and down to the far side, before it really breaks. If we have real bad weather here we'll never get across. It should be easy going, in fact I can see some sort of a path. The col isn't very high either. Come on. One big effort and we'll be over the far side."

Rory stood beside me with water dripping out of his sleeves.

"I want pancakes," he said. "I must have some pancakes. You promised me them."

"Oh, come on," I remonstrated, "there are much more important things to worry about now."

His young mind knew that he wanted something and he put all his discomforts of cold and wet and hunger into the one thought. Pancakes!

"Mum," he began to cry, "I want them now, this minute. You have to make them for me. I can't go any further without a pancake."

"I'll make you one at the far side. We'll find a nice place to camp beside the sea," I promised.

It was a stiff carry and with my head down I was not even aware of the blackness of the clouds. There was no view from the col, only a steep slither down through the undergrowth to the water's edge. The sea looked black and threatening and as we scrambled to erect the tent the storm broke, battering us with sleet and rain. What did the Vikings do in weather like this, I wondered. The Eskimos have their great capacity for switching off, for curling up in bad weather and hibernating.

The Vikings, though, would feel as I did now: wet, chilled to my very marrow.

"Where's the primus?" shouted Hugh from inside the tent.

"I don't know," I said, "I'm sure it was in the front of the canoe when we left." I looked around but couldn't see it anywhere. "It must have come," I said, "we can't have left it behind, surely."

My teeth were beginning to chatter now and I could see that Rona was blue in the face.

"Surely you didn't stuff it inside that big canvas bag," I said, seeing an oddly humped sack among our luggage. "If you put it in there the paraffin will be all over everything."

Cold and uncomfortable I got rid of my feelings by yelling at Hugh. Like Rory, who was still wailing on for his pancakes.

"Here it is," said Robin. "What's all the fuss about?"

He was showing far more resourcefulness than me. Remembering the last gale I now carefully placed boulders on every peg and anchored down the fly sheet.

"You promised, you promised," wailed Rory from inside. I was so tired I couldn't bear the thought of cooking anything, let alone the bloody pancakes. I crawled into the tent with the wind howling at my heels. The rain was lashing on the canvas, beating it down on one side.

"It must be frantic right out in the fjord," said Hugh. "We're really in a very sheltered place here. Couldn't be better for weathering out a storm."

10

THE PINK SWEET flesh of the salmon was absolutely delicious. The wind had been howling all night and the rain lashing against the tent. I was prepared to snuggle back into the sleeping bag and hibernate like the Eskimos. But not the children. Rory clambered over me yet again to look out.

"I can't even see the sea," he shouted, facing in the wrong direction. "It's absolutely black."

"I don't believe you," said Rona, shoving past him and allowing a great blast of rain and wind to come inside. The primus spurted with indignation. "He's right," she said letting the door fall back into place, "you can't see a thing. It's as if there's a grey curtain just at the edge of the shore there. You just can't see into it and yet it's only a few paces away."

"Go and get some water for tea," Hugh said to Robin.

"I'll get saturated, Dad," he answered indignantly.

"Well, take your clothes off then," I said. "I've done it before. It's the best thing in weather like this."

He did as I suggested and "streaked" out into the storm, clutching the blackened billy can. He was soon back.

"Didn't have to go far, there's a whole torrent pouring down the rocks just round there. There was no sign of a stream there yesterday when we arrived."

In Hugh's briefcase I had discovered a new Graham Greene and was longing to get back to it. I had just read the tantalizing statement, "The sexual and creative instinct live and die together," when a warm tide of wetness slurped onto the only remaining dry patch of my trousers. Hugh had upset the billy can.

"Just washing the paraffin off the ground sheet," he said in a cheery voice.

"Don't look so cross, Mum," said Rona.

"Do you think the Vikings would be friendly like the Eskimos or cross and frosty like the Danes," asked Rory.

I had wondered this myself. The Danes are not sure of themselves, clinging on to the marginal environment. And the ones that are find people like us a threat to their "splendid isolation" and an intrusion on their scene. Whereas the Eskimos, who are perfectly capable of living here for another 2,000 years, just love people. They will share anything and enjoy a new face and the excitement of strangers.

"They weren't always friendly," added Rory. "Remember the fights between the Vikings and the scraelings."

Rory loved turning the words over in his mouth.

"The scraelings would come creeping up in weather like this. The Vikings would be frightened, hiding in their turf houses."

"Actually," I said, "the Eskimos often preferred to settle arguments without shedding any blood. For instance," I said turning to Hugh, "they have a sort of competition where they tell long stories about their enemy. The purpose is to outdo him and make him look ridiculous. A song or long ballad is supported by beating the drum and when one person is finished at last, his opponent starts on his; and the first one to run out of words is the loser. There are very few stories of Eskimos actually killing off each other, although sometimes there was a blood feud. The record for murder in a family feud was a man who killed thirteen of his relations. It is interesting that the old legends of the Eskimos are usually not about fights with each other, or with the Vikings, but mostly concerning the struggle against the invincibility of their surroundings. The ocean, the ice, the animals and the wind and also, of course, the ghosts."

The supernatural powers that the Eskimo believed in were often friendly. They helped him struggle for his daily necessities. Every soul had its ally in the supernatural, even the weakest. The widows and orphans as well as the hunters, who were protected by spirits living among the rocks on the beach. If a kayaker died he would wake up again at the bottom of the sea where he would be received by his relations. A demon lived in the ocean too, but he was quite friendly, and often the kayakers encountered him and had long conversations.

Thinking of the old days, I wondered if I would rather have lived in the Viking long house, or the Eskimo round. The same amount of people lived in each. The Eskimos though, would be far warmer. Six to eight families together and the house heated by ten to twelve lamps, emitting such a heat that most people removed their clothes entirely.

An early traveller to Greenland describes the smell! He wrote that "they seldom wash and eat from the same vessels and bowls that the dogs have eaten from without cleaning them first. They eat lice and vermin from themselves and others. Nothing goes to waste. They scrape the sweat off their faces with a knife and lick it up. They are not at all ashamed to relieve themselves in the presence of others." The Vikings, on the other hand, were certainly quite keen on washing. And one of the earliest sagas states that "a guest should be met at the table by his host carrying water and a towel, as well as a hearty welcome". Later on, the same account says that "freshly washed and well filled with food should every man set off, even if he is not too well dressed". One of the days of the week—Saturday—was named as the day for washing. The old Norse name "*laugardagr*" means "bath". Cleanliness was also symbolic of Christianity and a certain mountain, believed holy, should not be looked at by an unwashed face.

A very different account is given of the Vikings who travelled to the east, who were described by the Arabs as extremely dirty. They were said to be "the most unclean of God's creatures who do not wash themselves after discharging their natural functions, nor even after a meal. They are as stray donkeys." In England though, the Vikings were described as being most careful of their appearance and even combed their hair and changed their linen frequently "in order the more easily to overcome the reluctance of women and procure the daughters of noblemen as their mistresses". The Vikings in Greenland would have the added difficulty of no soap. For washing their clothes, though, they would probably adopt the old Greenland habit of using urine which contained the valuable cleansing element, ammonia.

"Did the Vikings fight each other, though?" persisted Rory, bringing me back to the same subject.

"Well," I said, "we know that they had to abide by their principles of blood vengeance. Don't you remember, Erik the Red was thrown out of Norway for that very reason? There is another story of a man who travelled all the way to Greenland to avenge a killing that a local had committed at some time during a feud in Iceland. This man's revenge lasted for years, with him chasing his victim from settlement to settlement.

"It's interesting though that the sagas about Greenland itself never tell of inter-settlement feuds. The people here seem to have had a peaceful relationship with each other, and when fights are recorded their causes always prove to come from outside Greenland itself. The first settlers and their families seem to have formed a sort of ruling class and a special aura seems to have surrounded them, which nobody tried to usurp. Everyday life did not seem to call for any special protection. Their farms were scattered over a large area, as we know. They did not huddle together for protection. Living in isolation the people, though, would naturally feel unsafe in the company of strangers even if they spoke the same language."

Hugh looked more like a cave man, or a scraeling, than a Viking farmer. He squatted at the other side of the tent with his black hair all over his face and his beard an inch long already. Robin looked the perfect explorer type too, but Rona was running her fingers through her golden hair and looked quite spruce.

A world without sun is like a world without love, I thought, as a few hours later I peered out of the tent door at the gloomy scene. It was black, with here and there a slight relief of dark grey. There was no colour whatsoever. The wind had not abated and the rain squalls lashed at the tent.

"Might get better with the change in the tide," I said hopefully, coming back inside the tent.

"I'm going to make rum butter," announced Rona.

"Keep your hands off that," said Hugh, jumping up to protect the bottle.

"I only need a few drops," she added. "I thought I would use the fish fat in the bottom of the frying pan for butter. It'll be just great."

"I'd much rather drink it," I said hastily, snatching the bottle away myself. We whiled away the day, and woke in the morning to peace.

At 4 a.m. the sky was clearing to the north. By six it was clearing to the south. Little birds began to flutter about. We were up and away as the sun reached the tent. We were short of time now, and must reach the head of Igaliko Fjord that day.

Who could imagine this was the same world as that rent by the storm of yesterday? The sea was absolutely flat calm, real mirror stuff. We rounded the point into the main arm of the fjord. Still there was no ripple to break the surface. Close to the shore we now turned to face the north. Full of energy after our day's rest we passed quickly along the coast which soon fell away to the arm of the fjord leading to the west. The view there was of silvers and greys and sparkling white as the sun picked up the reflection from the snow. The view was for us to see twice over—completely reflected in the dead calm water. This was too good to be true.

"Let's cross now," I shouted to Hugh in the other canoe.

We knew that before the day was out we had to cross to the other shoreline and at this point the fjord was at its widest. But by crossing now we could cut down the distance.

"Okay," Hugh shouted back, turning his canoe and setting off out into the open water.

I spread the map out on my knees and pointed out to Robin that the headland diagonally up from us was called Nulup Nua.

"Let's stop there for lunch," I said looking at my watch. It was only 8 am. Cliffs swept down on the far side, sheer into the water and their steepness completely masked any view to the head of the fjord.

"Where is Igaliko?" said Robin. "You'd think we would have seen some sign of it by now. After all, quite a few people live there, don't they?"

"Yes," I answered, "but of course it isn't as important now as it used to be in the old days. With the Vikings it was the absolute centre of their whole life here in Greenland. That is of course after the place became Christian. The bishop lived at Igaliko although he actually called the place Gardar. There, according to the sagas, was the cathedral. They have found all sorts of things in graves there, a gold ring for instance, and a bishop's ivory staff."

Robin dipped his paddle into the thick greeny water of the fjord. We were close now to where fingers of ice dripped down from the glaciers, tinging the sea about us. It took no effort to move the canoe through the peaceful scene. Two hours' gentle paddling and we were there.

We scrambled up steep slithery rocks to a ledge formed between the cliffs of olivine basalt. Sea pinks were flourishing everywhere, and plantain with fleshy leaves. I threw myself down on the sage green leaves to soak up the sun. It was absolutely marvellous. I could feel the stiffness caused by the damp wet sog of the last few days recovering as the rays penetrated every pore.

"Ten miles already," said Robin again looking at the map. "I'm dead hungry. It's lunch time, you know."

I looked at my watch. "Oh it isn't. Surely we can go a bit further. We haven't *got* any lunch, anyway."

"I'll go and catch a fish then," he said moving already.

He scrambled down to the canoe and was soon sitting in it slightly off-shore, peering below.

"Do you want a big one or the sweeter small kind?" he said leaning overboard. "There's one here with a very big head which looks quite good, but on the other hand there are several small, fat ones."

He moved the hook at the end of the line from side to side as he decided which fish to select for lunch.

"I'll cook them," said Hugh, "I want them really crisp on the outside. You always make them so soggy."

I lay back again in the sun and did not stir until the scent of frying fish wafted in my direction. I did not want to move on. I could not bear the thought of arriving. Reaching Igaliko signified the end of our journey. After that it was a question of a very steep and long portage and we would be back to Erik's fjord with a view of where we had started from. I wanted to prolong this nomadic way of life for ever. Here our priorities were whether there was food for supper and what the weather was like. Whereas soon we would be back into the question of money and jobs, deadlines and responsibilities.

The children, though, were avid to keep moving. They longed for anything new and the thought of a settlement with people meant to them a new experience and all the excitement that went with it.

"The tide's come in," said Rona. "If we don't move quickly the canoes will be washed away."

It was only that remark that got me to my feet and reluctantly I followed the rest as they packed up and pushed the canoes off. We rounded the point and still there was nothing to see ahead. The sun scorched down on us and the sea was still flat calm. Another hour and some small little houses came into focus on pink rock. We drew nearer and I could make out the shape of men. I began to long for a beer; it was so hot.

"What are the people doing?" asked Robin, turning round. "I can't make it out at all. They seem to be busy about something between those rocks down near the shore."

The men had seen us and now we heard the call "Kayakers" passing from mouth to mouth as it was picked up from one group of people to the next. I began to feel a thrill of excitement as we saw small black shapes running down towards the rocks.

"Where do you think the harbour is?" asked Robin again. "It's just sheer cliff there. We can't possibly land."

"Must be round the corner," I answered.

Now we were passing right below the black rock. The people were jumping up and down talking to each other and shouting encouraging words to us. What a welcome! Now they began to cheer. There were Eskimos everywhere and as we came round the corner and saw a little shingle beach, the people ran into the sea and actually picked us up in the canoe and bore us ashore still sitting inside our boats! They set us down high above the tide mark and gathered round. I was handed a can of beer and thankfully I lifted it to my lips and gulped it down. Only then did I look around at the people who were so excited at our arrival.

To my surprise all the faces were of pure Eskimo: high cheek bones, oriental eyes and inky black hair. They smiled constantly, giving an aura of happiness and genuine joy and pleasure at us being there. It was as if they were thrilled to see our adaptation to their old way of life, a life that they were told so often nowadays was out of date and archaic. Yet here we were: Mum, Dad and a group of children absolutely at one with our surroundings and doing what they would enjoy. They could never quite understand what the Danes were about. They expended energy on what seemed unnecessary pursuits. Like building complicated houses, ridiculously big boats, or making far more clothes than you could wear at once. What was the point of it all?

By now I had drunk several cans of beer and looking round realized that so had Robin, to say nothing of Rory! He was being handled from arm to arm by all the women who had gathered, making a great fuss of his hair. Everybody wanted a shot in our canoes. I sat on the shingle beach and watched the excitement. We had not unpacked our gear, but I had drunk too much beer to really worry as the canoes were pulled over the stones and people stepped in and out. Our feathering of the paddle caused much merriment. The older men could not understand why the blades did not match, but the younger ones were quicker on the uptake and soon had the canoes speeding across the fjord at a fantastic rate. Sure enough, the kayaks of the old days could easily make a speed of ten to fifteen knots or even more. In all kinds of weather it was still faster and more reliable than the motor boat.

I looked around me at the strange cross fertilization of the stone age and modern sophisticated Scandinavia. The children about me were born to Kamiks and sealskin as well as to rubber boots and cotton, a complete mixture of old and new, rich and poor, from a barter economy to money. The jump was a big one and very difficult. Will the Danish welfare save the people, or will it make them incapable of standing up to the lost world which is their home? The weather, after all, has not changed. "Investing in people" became a slogan in Greenland politics some years ago. Any young Greenlander can get loans from the State for whatever type of education he wishes no matter what the price. There are fishing factories, technical schools and more than 1,000 children are sent to Denmark every year for higher education. But would the people rather be dressed in European-type clothes and aim at a job in a State shop or study in Denmark? Which world do they want, or how will they know what it is they want? The men now having such fun in our canoes became motorized several years ago, leaping from their own kayak to a small cutter, obtained almost without down payment from the government. I noticed a young woman watching the excitement but hard at work sitting on the rocks above the little bay. She was scraping a skin with her ulu, or oval-shaped blade. There was nothing motorized about her. She was holding the skin between her teeth while scraping it clean of blubber. Her hands moved quick as lightning. No machine could do the job better.

Hugh was becoming agitated about the canoes. The next time one came ashore to change paddlers, he indicated that it was time for us to move. Everyone helped lift them up onto the level ground outside a big shed above us. This was the KGH store. In a minute all our belongings were alongside and all our new friends escorted us into the shop. As usual, there was one clever girl with a smattering of English.

"A man with a horse wishes to help you to carry over to Igaliko Fjord," she said with perfect diction.

Rory was astounded that this Eskimo could speak his language. He gazed at her with fascination. Armed with beer of our own we repaired to the steps outside the shop to treat our new friends. Sitting there with the sun in my face I now took a closer look at the settlement of Igaliko.

Where are the Viking ruins? The very best ones were supposed to be here somewhere.

"There's a ruin," said Rory pointing to a perfectly neat trim little house close by. I realized what he meant. The walls were of beautifully turned stone exactly similar to what we had seen at Hvalsey.

"It isn't that the Vikings have lived there," I said to Rory, "it's modern people removing the stones from the old ruins to build their own houses. Not that that looks so new. I expect it's about 200 years old."

The people had been gathering hay between the rocks. Everyone was out. It was a communal effort. Sheep wandered about between the snug little houses and I could see now that they were all made of stone gleaned from the Viking's walls. I thought I had seen it all before.

It was a scene from the Western Isles of Scotland perhaps 100 years ago. South Harris was like this. Common grazing land. Common jobs and a common share out of what nature provided. The people weren't rivals. They were part of the community which helped everyone stumble along. You could not draw ahead of the rest, but nor could you drop too far behind. There was nothing much to strive for and certainly no Joneses to try to keep up with.

The people wanted to know where we had been, and Robin and Hugh were both busy drawing a sketch on the steps with a piece of stone of the various fjords that we had crossed. More people were peering at the map and there was much chat about us, where we had come from and where we were going. Then I noticed that galloping towards us wildly and completely out of control was a little pony with a driftwood cart. The people were all talking at us now and I gathered that this was the man who had come to take us over the hill. In a great shower of dust the cart juddered to a halt beside us, and a man jumped down from the shaft. He spoke in an extraordinary way and I could not understand a word. He had a cleft palate. His pronunciation and Eskimo were too much for me. So it was a question of nodding our heads and waving our hands about in all directions. He was very alert and quick on the uptake and soon understood that we didn't want to leave at once but preferred to find the Viking ruins.

Word went around, and the whole village now rose to its feet and started to escort us between the little houses of pink stone.

"Isn't it just like South Harris?" I said to Hugh.

"Yes," he said, "but with one exception. Look at the virility and vigour of the men. Young and old. Everyone is busy. Do you see? And just look at what they're doing. All those blades of grass are being manicured to make hay for the winter. When did you last see anyone working as hard as that at home?"

The houses looked snug and welcoming. Was this the way the Vikings lived, I thought? These after all were the only stone houses in the whole of Greenland. Perhaps it was similar to South America where no one seems to have made any innovations since the Incas. There the irrigation system, the laws of the land, the terrace cultivation and the methods of looking after the animals have not changed for hundreds of years.

We'd all stopped outside one of the houses. It belonged to the owner of the cart—the man with the cleft palate. He beckoned us in and we had to bend to get below the lintel. I looked around and felt that the clock had stopped at the turn of the last century. This house was not Eskimo, or Danish, but Greenland. A complete mixture of the two cultures blended into a definite style.

I was able by now to understand the strange diction of my friend with the cleft palate. We sat down round his table to more beer and asked him about the Vikings. I knew that this narrow isthmus separating Erik's Fjord from Igaliko Fjord was the site of the homestead of Erik the Red's illegitimate daughter Freydis and her half-brother and husband Thorvald who were reported to be very wealthy. The couple, though, were ill-thought of by everybody. She was the one involved in the feud in America. It is not known how long they lived here, nor whether they had any children to take over the farm; but it is known that this site had the best grazing facilities in the entire Viking settlement and because of that it was fixed upon as the site for the bishop's seat. The land was sold to the Church, which caused a lot of trouble as no place quite as good could be alloted to the owner.

Erik the Red's wife's church had been the first in Greenland, but with the spread of Christianity the need for churches had naturally sprung up in all the other areas. The clergy who came from Scandinavia, were always complaining that none had been properly consecrated by a bishop, nor had the ground in which they buried their dead. What would happen at the end of the world to those whose bodies had been buried in unconsecrated ground? The local churchmen felt that they could not take upon themselves such a responsibility. Nor could they perform confirmations in a church that did not belong to any bishop's see. None of the important elements that formed the core of the church ceremonies could be solemnly consecrated. In mediaeval Europe, it will be remembered, the slightest alteration of a church made it useless if it were not immediately reconsecrated; which shows how often the Greenland ministers must have had to compromise with their conscience. The clergy were very much answerable to their bishop and were not supposed to take any initiative. They were supposed to turn to him constantly and in Greenland they felt completely cut off without this spiritual mentor as well as feeling a complete lack of authority to administer the tithes and donations that were the core of the Church's economy.

The churches in Greenland, of course, were always built on land belonging to a farmer, who had a sort of patronage over the new buildings, and it was recognized that he had rights to the tithes offered up by the peasants who used it. This followed the pattern of the rest of Scandinavia where the Church was far from being independent. The local ministers could not cope with the difficulties of this policy, and began to implore the Catholic Church at home to send them a bishop. The local people began to see that they needed one too and so decided that one of the young men on the settlements, Einar Sokkason, should be commissioned to go to Norway to try to find one for Greenland. He sailed directly and was well received by the King, who listened to Einar and agreed.

After quickly considering a suitable candidate the King decided to send for Arnald who was a good priest and would make an excellent bishop. Arnald was not at all happy at the prospect. His first objection was that he was not good enough for the job but then admitted that he did not want to leave friends and relatives. His final plea was that he was "hopeless at handling difficult people". The King answered that the more difficulties Arnald overcame the greater would be the reward in heaven. He listened to no more objections and set about seeing that Arnald received all the various consecrations that the Church considered necessary. After all these matters had been seen to, Einar presented the King with a white polar bear that he had brought specially from Greenland. The date was 1125. They had a bad journey back, being forced to seek shelter in Iceland where they remained the winter. Eventually, though, they sailed up the fjord and reached Erik the Red's farm by which time it had been decided to establish the see at Gardar. A church was built on an impressive site commanding a view down the fjord. Behind, the ground rose steeply to the col over to the west. The bishop's house faced east and the fjord.

Excavations carried out in 1926 revealed an impressive group of buildings that comprised Arnald's see. His settlement was dominated by the cathedral which he dedicated to St Nicholas, the patron saint of sea-farers. It seemed on his arrival Bishop Arnald must have ordered an extension and partial rebuilding of the church that had been prepared for him. He also extended the farm which he took over. He apparently felt that the circumstances and surroundings of the bishop had to be stately! He also needed space for carrying out his official duties as it was his responsibility to see to the law of the land. He needed a large domestic staff for running his establishment. He also insisted on a bell tower and this was built in the south-eastern corner of the courtyard around the church.

It took Arnald a few years to finish the improvements on his ceremonial hall but when it was completed it was said by a writer of the sagas that "It was only surpassed by a single hall in Iceland". So the bishop was certainly able to entertain his guests. Their faces would have been lit by the flames of the log fire burning in the great pit which also would send flickering light up into the roof, to create shadows among the rafters. The walls were covered by tapestries in narrow strips with the decoration carefully kept at eye level in a long mural. Several hundred people could have fitted in to this great hall.

Looking out of the window of the Greenlander's house I could see across to two great doorways standing among the ruins.

"Let's go and look," said Rory jumping up, noticing the direction in which I had been looking. Cleft Palate stood up and indicated that he would show us what there was to be seen. A long passage led to the great hall from the front of the old Viking house. I realized I was standing on an enormous stone flag, the weight of which must have been at least ten tons.

"Look how those flags have been worn hollow," pointed out Hugh looking down at the sandstone paving of the passage.

Actually three paved paths led from here towards the church.

"This is for the cows," shouted Robin from a long building further to the left. "The men say it could hold 107 of them. I've counted the stones dividing the stalls and I think they must be right. We haven't seen anything nearly as big as this in all the other ruins."

I could see that Robin's building was constructed of large fan-shaped blocks forming a cavity wall which must have been filled with earth and turf. More turf was padded on the outside to keep out the wind.

"They must have used a lot of hay," said Rory looking around at the small patches of grass that were growing today.

"Yes, and that's where they kept it I suppose," I said, pointing to what seemed to be a storeroom.

"Remember," said Hugh, "they weren't just faced with the problems of storing their own hay but they would also have to have somewhere to keep the tithes."

This was the name given to the fees paid by the people to the Church. Some of the goods would have to be shipped out, because the bishops had not only to collect tithes for themselves but also for the Church at Rome. These would be the so called "Peter's Pence" which were used to finance their crusades. As no mediaeval coins have been unearthed in any of the Norse farms in Greenland it is supposed that the people paid all their tithes in kind. The goods then had to be sold, which meant that the Church officials had to carry on a "business". And the Gardar bishop was faced with the added difficulty that he could not be sure that his goods would be shipped off each year to Scandinavia. As I looked around this site I couldn't help thinking that perhaps the profusion of buildings was not a proof of the success of the Church in Greenland but more of Arnald's abilities as a business man. The tithes from Greenland were sent first to Norway, where they were then sent on to Rome. One of the collectors for Norway reported that on 1 August 1327 he received the tithes of the Greenland see, which were paid in kind with 127 stone of walrus ivory. The whole consignment was sold in Flanders for £12; half the sum was payable to the Norwegian king and the remaining valued at 114 gold florins, which is more than 400 grams of pure gold. This weight of walrus ivory is that of about 373 tusks.

It is interesting that walrus ivory was the most important commodity to the Norse settlers in Greenland. The Church considered it fair payment because the ivory was so much in demand in Europe. It is possible that other payments for the Church were converted into walrus tusks and that Arnald set up as a large scale exporter of the ivory. This is probably the explanation for the small groups of foraging hunters who seemed to have left the Viking settlements and travelled north. Runic stones have been found as far north as the 73rd parallel and these hunters were apparently accompanied by the Church on their strenuous hunting expeditions. There is an account dating from the latter half of the thirteenth century indicating that the hunters had ventured even further north than usual and that later in the year the Church sent a ship to collect the tusks. This was driven off course but the sailors succeeded in steering their way out of the mist and when they finally sighted land it had "many glaciers and seals and white bears".

On the return voyage the night temperature is reported to have dropped below zero on 25 July and the crew caught a glimpse of the midnight sun. It was also stated that they found traces of scraelings. From closely reading this report it appears that it was the Church that instigated the expedition. It seems that the Church was a good mixture of the spiritual and temporal "interests"!

Cleft Palate wanted us to move on to see the graveyard. He

was shouting and waving his arms at us to hurry up. As we walked over I reminded the children that the bishop's grave had been dug up here and that the skeleton had a gold ring on the right ring finger, with a staff of carved walrus ivory in his hand.

Rory had gone in the other direction.

"There's a bridge here, Mum. Did you know that the Vikings built bridges?"

I could see that he was standing near a dyke of stone and turf—a fenced-in field—and that his bridge was actually a dam, perhaps used for irrigation purposes. There would be little snow on this narrow strip of land between the two fjords and so no water reservoirs in the mountains for the summer months. A woman now came out of one of the nearby houses carrying a bucket. I saw her walk over to close beside the graveyard and kneel down to fill it from a well. We looked closely at this spring and saw that the stone edging around was undoubtedly of Norse origin. I felt that the Vikings would have been pleased to see the woman carry the water from their well back to her house made of stones taken from their buildings. Her clothes were not all that different either. Some well preserved items of clothing have been found in a churchyard further south, showing that the people wore a home-spun robe-like garment, with a hood which hung down the back in a tassel. They wore long stockings underneath. The clothes that were found were worn, patched, working garments corresponding closely to those of mediaeval Europe. I wanted to see more, but Cleft Palate felt we must be on the move. He was jostling us all back towards his house where he caught his horse once more and we all followed him down at a run back to the KGH store.

All our belongings were tossed into the cart, made of pieces of wood nailed together in a haphazard fashion. The canoes were carefully lifted up and placed on top. Hugh was just about to secure them with a piece of rope when the cart set off at a run. Two dogs were snapping at the horse's hooves and there was nothing for it but to follow. I was soon puffing and panting a long way behind. The villagers shouted and waved but I could do nothing but concentrate on trying to keep up. Without a sideways glance I ran past the rest of the Viking ruins. The children had not even seen them! They were clustered round the cart like flies.

Thank heavens the path out of the village took to the steepest part of the hill, and soon the cart was forced to slow down. Sweating I managed to reach them.

"The horse has got a name," said Rona. "It's called Hellman Heinz."

"How do you know?" I said.

"Well the man keeps saying that when I ask him," said Rona.

Hugh chipped in. "His pronunciation is so bizarre it could actually be anything."

"Hellman Heinz," I said friendlily to the pony, at which it kicked up its heels and tore off again at high speed with Cleft Palate and the rest of us tearing along as best we could. At least the horse wanted to go in the same direction, I thought as I tottered up the rough track. No question of looking at the view or thinking of the Vikings. I stumbled on blindly, sweat now stinging my eyes. Gasping for breath at last I collided with the back of the cart. It had come to a halt on the col.

Ahead we could see Erik's Fjord. I felt a great surge of relief and satisfaction. We had made it. Cleft Palate had by now lifted Rory aboard and he sat perched on top of the canoes. He indicated that the others should get on too. So I gave Rona a hand.

"He means you as well," said Robin.

Sure enough he was offering to give me a hitch up alongside the kids. I had just tentatively got two feet onto the edge of the cart and was considering whether I should really climb up when the pony was off. Clutching anything I could, my feet flailing the air, I lay spreadagled as we tore down the path at breakneck speed. Every time I lifted my head the wind rushed into my eyes. I could see nothing. All I could do was cling on like mad.

The mad rush stopped at last and I gingerly lifted my head before falling off the cart. I was sitting on a stretch of macha close to the shore and as I looked up I saw a huge iceberg. It felt like home. It was the first ice we had seen in many days.

Cleft Palate was now digging below our load and produced yet more beer. This time I really needed it! We downed a couple of cans and then shook hands all round. We all said goodbye to Hellman Heinz who suddenly decided that it was time to go and at his usual speed of "as fast as possible" set off at another gallop, Cleft Palate rushing along behind, shouting.

11

A HUGE GLACIER spewed its ice into the sea at the head of Erik's Fjord close to our point. Round this and we knew we would be among the 'bergs.

The ice crashed and bashed all night. I hardly slept. How were we going to get through? Between us and the airstrip a finger of the Greenland Ice Cap touched down into the sea, moving all the time. Millions of tons of ice are cast off daily into the water. Time was running out. We could not wait for the wind and tide to disperse the icebergs and brash that seemed to be completely blocking the route. The storm of a few days ago must have created this chaos. Would there be a route through for our vulnerable canoes or would we be forced out into the main expanse of the fjord where we would have to cope with its tide race amd funnelling winds which would catch us miles off shore at a moment's notice?

The others were clustering round the fire outside when at last I woke up in the morning. I was still tired after my restless sleep and felt too the pace had slackened now that we were in this fjord. I looked out to a low Scotch mist clearing slightly to the south as a silver grey light.

"What do you think?" I asked Hugh, "should we go?"

"Well," he said, "we haven't got the time not to have a go. I think we should push off for a recce. Let's get out of this sheltered bay anyway, and see what's ahead."

I slowly packed up and as I rolled up the sleeping bag I realized that our journey was far from over. We still had the most significant part to go. This ice would be the real test for the canoes. However, I tried to convince myself, it is the kayak that is used to get through the ice to this day by many Greenlanders who could use a motor boat but find the older craft able to navigate in places that the larger boat cannot.

We paddled out of our secluded bay. I peered ahead at the

sun sparkling off a wall of white. Hugh was ahead, canoeing towards it. The scenery was fantastically beautiful. Blue icebergs were on our left and others as clear as glass all around. There was a noise of constant bells tinkling and then the "thump" as a large 'berg collapsed.

"Tide's changing," said Robin. "That's why the 'bergs are on the move. Look at the speed that that one's going."

He was pointing towards a block of ice that seemed to me to be moving faster than us.

"Keep seaway on your left," shouted back Hugh, pointing to the ice that was now closing in behind.

I looked ahead. Was there a route through to the far shore? It certainly didn't look too far. We zig-zagged a course through the ice lying in our path. Each 'berg seemed more beautiful. They were perfectly reflected in the calm water. There was utter peace. The ice seemed benign and stable. It enchanted us on. I was heading now for a channel between two lines of 'bergs. We were certainly sheltered from the wind and the water was so calm because the effect of floating ice is to dampen down any movement on the surface. As I reassured myself I became more aware of the 'bergs further out moving at quite a fast speed and I realized that the tide and breeze could move them so that our safe passage could suddenly shut behind us.

Then, suddenly, over my shoulder I glimpsed movement. A huge 'berg was heading for us, fast.

"Paddle," I yelled at Robin. It was travelling faster than us, occupying all the space and our access to the open sea.

"It's rolling over," shrieked Robin, his arms flaying the air as he paddled frantically.

We surged forward surfing down a huge swell in its shadow. The canoe juddered. I thought it had hit us. We swayed to one side. I had no control over the rudder—but we were upright. Only our rear end had touched the 'berg. All was still. Utter silence and tranquillity once more. Had it really happened? I could see the others still ahead, completely unconcerned. All was still.

Instead of frightened I now felt strangely at home. The canoe seemed completely master of the environment. It *was* the only craft able to pass through, as the Eskimos knew of old. The ice ahead seemed thicker again. Was there a way? Too late to turn back. We were trapped. No, there was just a chink between two large 'bergs. The far shore now seemed quite close but the ice was piled up on the submerged rocks just off shore. I could see a lateral moraine coming down to meet the sea in a point making a secluded bay on either side. I headed for this. Hugh was not making for the shore but was, in fact, canoeing to and fro and round the ice, supremely happy.

We were through. I paddled for the shingle below the terminal moraine and beached the canoe. I stepped out onto the grey shingle. There was no room to camp at this level but as I clambered up the loose stones I could see that a perfect camp site was formed by the angle of the moraine to the cliff. In this sunken hollow I threw myself down and peering out had a bird's eye view of the scene. A silver sky with cumulus clouds which were tossed up into great cathedrals by the catabatic wind. A rock garden was at my feet, all the alpine flowers I could think of were flourishing between the pink granite boulders. The glacier must have picked up all the minerals and brought them along to toss out on this little niche. On the cliff itself I could see a scarlet patch of rose root. The seasons had changed. When we had set off down Erik's Fjord the plant had been a fleshy green. Now it was autumn.

Hugh was clambering up the loose gravel behind me.

"Not much driftwood."

"No," I agreed, "but I can see a lot of low juniper bushes further up the moraine. There seems to be much dead wood among them."

Sure enough, we soon all gathered handfuls, taking care not to spike ourselves on the sharp leaves of this little shrub. Our tent took up most of our little eyrie. There was just room for a fire between us and the slope.

"I have never been in such a fantastic place," I said to Hugh as I crouched down beside the smokey fire. "Oh, there's no water," I shouted to Robin suddenly remembering.

"That's all right Mum," he said, "I'll just go and catch an iceberg."

He glissaded down the moraine and was soon throwing stones at a piece that had broken off a large 'berg, to drive it ashore.

The sky was magnificent. It seemed to occupy far more space than normal. It glowed with light. The sea spread out below us uniting and separating the fingers of land. Man seemed quite unimportant. There was a great feeling, though, of time lasting endlessly behind us and also in front. The present day seemed quite immaterial. I felt that man had only entered this world quite recently and would just as soon depart. Two or three thousand million years seemed to have passed since this scene began. I had the impression as I stood there, that the scant layers of earth, sand and gravel, which the erosion of centuries had left lying in valleys and gorges and bays around us were tied by the roots of grass and creeping plants. Here and there moss and lichen had found holds on stones and rocks. It was as if, as the ice retreated further into the interior of the country, there was a tide of green that slowly crept along the shores, but retained a respectful distance from the Inland Ice. I could see that it was the sun that gave life and vigour to the land about us; without the sun it was dead. Flora on dry land came rapidly as soon as conditions permitted. Man came much later. Eskimo man though can tread lightly across his world. He doesn't ask for much and in return he takes little. For himself and his family a reindeer here or a fish there is all that he requires. The Eskimos were only hunting for themselves. They had no superstructure to which they had to pay homage or help to support. The Vikings on the other hand were quite different. Why should the walrus of West Greenland die to pay for the weapons for the crusaders, fighting a war that was completely unintelligible to the man in whose land it belonged?

"Are you thinking of the Vikings?" asked Rona sitting down beside me. "What do you think happened to them then? Where was the last one? Did he die here do you think?"

"I think they just ran out of their resources," I said. "In one farm that was excavated recently, a man's body was found lying in a passage leading from one room to the next. It was in a lovely site near a little lake. When I read about it I thought of that man, the only one left in the farm, wandering about from room to room in his old house. He was perhaps the last person left, for, with all the others dead, who was going to dig a grave for him? The animals must have died one by one, each body serving as food for the next until that one man had nothing left to eat and, weakened and sick, wandered about the house until he died there in his own passage."

Hugh had joined us.

"I remember a letter that I read of a sea captain whose boat visited Greenland in 1540. He said he had sailed into a fjord through a narrow channel and that his crew noticed that the land was inhabited so they went ashore. They found boathouses and byres very similar to those found in Iceland, and on the beach there was a dead man, clothed in a coat made of homespun and seal skin. He had a hood over his head and was clutching a knife which had been sharpened so often that there was little of the blade left. They described the man as having died exhausted by nature that had reared up against him. The captain said it was as if the lonely survivor fell to the ground in the final liberation of death. "It was as if," I said, "the summer was over. It was as if it was time to go home."

"Don't be so gloomy," interrupted Robin. "We've got several days left and a good few miles still to go."

We gathered more driftwood and spent the evening sitting round the fire. It was a clear dark-blue sky above, lit by stars. As we watched the full orb of the moon slowly rose out of the mountains below Igaliko and climbed into the cold clear sky. It hung there and from behind it suddenly there appeared curtains of light. They vanished as if rubbed out. They re-appeared brighter then faded. Once more, coming and going, rising and falling with no rhythm, but a strange constancy.

"It's the Northern Lights," I explained to Rory. "I have seen them coloured some times at home."

"They're magic," he whispered, sitting mesmerized by the strange rise and fall of the light in the sky. Now our world began to fill with noise. The tide must have changed and the ice began crashing and bashing together. There was not enough room for it all. The 'bergs rode up on top of each other then collapsed with a roar, smashed onto the shore and colliding with more 'bergs piling up behind. A slow mist was creeping in from the sea and soon the whole mystery of the night was blotted out.

When I peered over the wall formed by the moraine in the morning it was into a steel-grey world. The horizons were close with the mist, but below the bay was full of ice. The scene was as if bleached, no colour but for the shades of white in the 'bergs. Reluctantly we struck camp and carried everything down the steep bank to load up the canoes once more. Close to, the ice had all the colours of green and blue as well as white. A 'berg collapsed off shore. There was a splash but little wave.

Round the final spur of moraine the glacier was hidden. Our view ahead was towards a dark cliff that we knew hid the airstrip of Narssarssuaq from our view. It began to rain, real heavy wetting blobs that thudded down on the canvas. The wind crept up from behind. We pushed on past our very first camp. The dark rain clouds seemed to accentuate the bright greens of the herb slopes between the rocks on our right. The angelica seemed lusher than ever. Now I could see something red ahead. It was the oil depot at the harbour of the airstrip. Three more hours paddling and we had arrived.

The shacks of the little port seemed thrown together. The Eskimos, I thought, would learn less from modern European culture than in the days of their grandfathers and the Vikings. Or had our world something to offer them, I wondered, as there was a noise overhead and a great jet swooped down out of the sky. It picked us up like the eagle had its fish and soared us back across the ice cap and the sea to Europe. In a few more hours I sank into the hot spring pool in Iceland to wash off five week's of grime. Absolute bliss. Only my head poked out to be freshened by the rain. Rory was shouting something at me. I swam lethargically to the shore at the side of the pool to hear.

"They've got real lavatory seats you know!" he exclaimed.

That was all that had struck him about the return to civilization.